Praise for
The One-Page Project Manager

From Boise to Beijing, Clark Campbell's *One-Page Project Manager* has helped managers take complex tasks and reduce them to their most efficient core activities. If you are looking to maximize talent, time, and dollars *The One-Page Project Manager* is a MUST HAVE for your team.

> —Chester Elton
> Best-Selling Author
> *Managing with Carrots: The 24-Carrot Manager*

When managing large projects it is easy to lose oneself in gritty details only to wake up and realize that you spent valuable time on the wrong issues. In *The One-Page Project Manager,* Clark Campbell reveals a wonderful tool for keeping projects on task. Only one glance and we see the big issues requiring attention. It's the perfect organizational solution for the executive needing relevant project information.

> —Taylor Randall, PhD
> Professor
> David Eccles School of Business
> University of Utah

While at initial glance this book may appear to be simply about developing a "dashboard" for tracking an important project, it soon becomes clear that it is much more than that. The approach outlined by Clark Campbell, an experienced and accomplished project leader, provides a proven process for project management that significantly improves the chances that the project will be completed on time, on budget, and on target for its intended purposes. Furthermore, it provides a straightforward yet compelling set of steps to ensure that those with the ability and responsibility to achieve the desired results are supported, guided, and focused in their efforts to do so. This approach will prove especially beneficial to students and practitioners who want to learn and apply the skills and tools of effective project leadership.

> —Steven C. Wheelwright, PhD
> Baker Foundation Professor
> Senior Associate Dean
> Director of Publications Activities
> Harvard Business School
> Harvard University

Impressive in its simplicity, yet universal in its application, *The One-Page Project Manager* began assisting Chinese project managers in 2003, when Mr. Campbell first lectured in Beijing. OPPM is easy to learn and use, and is impressive in its clear capacity to communicate. It should be required reading for every manager who wants to improve project performance, accurately tell their story, and do it efficiently.

—Jonathan H. Du, PhD
CEO and Chairman
WiseChina Training Ltd.
Beijing, China

Communication may be the single most important critical success factor in project management. I have served as a CIO in 6 high-technology companies over the past 26 years. In this capacity, I have observed many successful, and unsuccessful, projects—including a very successful $30 million SAP/ERP implementation that I participated in using *The One-Page Project Manager*. This tool really works! It makes the complex look simpler, facilitates accurate and honest assessments, and all on just one page—which can, and will be, read by even the busiest executive.

—David C. Berg
Retired Chief Information Officer
IBM, Unisys and Sun Microsystems

As you read through Clark Campell's book, you will say to yourself, "so simple, yet intuitive and useful; I can put this to work today!" IT projects require meticulous attention to balancing scope, time, and resources. And the most important factor in successfully maintaining this equilibrium is communication, which *The One-Page Project Manager* delivers. Use *The One-Page Project Manager* and your projects will better deliver tasks to your objectives and stay closer to timelines and budgets, while facilitating critical ownership and engagement.

—Todd Thompson
Senior Vice President and Chief Information Officer
JetBlue Airways

THE ONE-PAGE PROJECT MANAGER

COMMUNICATE AND MANAGE ANY PROJECT WITH A SINGLE SHEET OF PAPER

CLARK A. CAMPBELL

BICENTENNIAL
1807
WILEY
2007
BICENTENNIAL

John Wiley & Sons, Inc.

Published by John Wiley & Sons, Inc., Hoboken, New Jersey.
Published simultaneously in Canada.

For general information on our other products and services or for technical support, please contact our Customer Care Department within the United States at (800) 762-2974, outside the United States at (317) 572-3993 or fax (317) 572-4002.

Wiley also publishes its books in a variety of electronic formats. Some content that appears in print may not be available in electronic books. For more information about Wiley products, visit our web site at www.wiley.com.

Library of Congress Cataloging-in-Publication Data:

Campbell, Clark. A., 1949–
   The one-page project manager : communicate and manage any project with a single sheet of paper / Clark. A Campbell.
      p.   cm.
   Includes bibliographical references and index.
   ISBN-13: 978-0-470-05237-2 (pbk.)
   ISBN-10: 0-470-05237-6 (pbk.)
1. Project management.   2. Business report writing.   I. Title.
   HD69.P75C363   2007
   658.4'04—dc22

                                                        2006015380

Printed in the United States of America.

15   14   13   12   11

To Meredith

CONTENTS

DOWNLOADABLE FORMS

Clark Campbell has written this book to help you manage your work better. He is sharing an amazing organizing format and the secrets of his successful management of many projects over the past 10 years—projects ranging from the simple to the bet-the-company variety. Whether your project is physical or intellectual, technical or plain, extensive or finite, this book helps you get your arms around it and organize your people to get it done the right way.

Who are "you"? A project manager, a functional vice president, a business unit leader, a CEO, any person with the responsibility to get something done or to manage the process. You will find the *One-Page Project Manager* (OPPM) to be an indispensable tool that you turn to repeatedly. OPPM provides an instantly visible one-page project picture showing objectives, time lines, responsibilities, allocation of resources, delegations, costs, and dependencies. OPPM has drill-down backup for those in the thick of the project, harmonizing all aspects of the collaborative work. While more involved schemes of project management are required for projects of immense complexity, even those can be reported up the chain using OPPM.

OPPM provides a unifying discipline enabling the project manager to envision what is to be done and how to go about it. In fact, its primary value lies in requiring the thought processes necessary to preparing the OPPM. For the executive sponsor or leader, its immense value lies in instant communication of project status.

In the mid-1990s, we became concerned about the quality of collaborative work in the company. We found that people could go off in inconsistent directions, working diligently on initiatives that ultimately conflicted with other initiatives, or didn't fit with existing processes. Lost opportunity costs were a real concern as well. To remedy the situation, we hired a project management trainer from the American Management Association to teach all our executives and managers the art and science of project management. Then we had a team led by Clark Campbell distill the training into an O.C. Tanner project management methodology. It was a valiant effort, but we soon ended up in project paper up to our ears, with boilerplate language throughout. Gleaning any information of value, making informed decisions, or knowing what was going on, was possible only with serious study of all of the papers and long question and answer sessions. Needless to say, we shelved the project management system before it shelved us.

Then a breakthrough happened. Clark devised OPPM and used it to construct a $10 million distribution center for our company. The project had four main aspects to it—the building, the computer system and applications, the automated storage and retrieval systems, and the work processes of distribution. Clark assigned each aspect to a manager, and each of them used OPPM for their specific work. Clark gave me a weekly OPPM update of all aspects of the project during the year of its duration. After a week or two, I gained the ability to *glance* at the OPPM and be brought up to date on all significant progress, problems, or dependencies. Our proj-

ect discussions became short, to the point, and focused on essential elements of the work. As President, I was also able to report to the CEO and our board of directors about the project in a knowledgeable, current, and thorough fashion without any help from actual project managers. Being ultimately responsible for the success of the project, I found that the use of OPPM made sponsoring the project a pleasure instead of a burden.

And so it has gone for the past 10 years. Whether the project was changing the legacy computer system for an entirely new one, or revamping our invoicing and accounts receivable collections, or developing new software-based products, OPPM has proved to be an organizing tool of great worth.

There are two things you can do to improve your project management discipline—hire Clark Campbell, or read his book and put OPPM in use. The first won't work—Clark isn't for hire. I recommend that you try the second without delay.

KENT H. MURDOCK
Chief Executive Officer
O.C. Tanner Company

Project management, like engineering or writing, is a discipline that requires the head, the heart, and years of experiences in order to embed the necessary essential engaging elements into one's bones. I am deeply grateful to many for providing platforms for nurturing and then maturing these attributes.

So it is with profound gratitude that I express appreciation to these colleagues, friends, teachers, and associates:

To Kent Murdock for trusting me with projects, and encouraging me to write this book.

To Dave Petersen, Wayne Carlston, Klaus Goeller, and Dennis Smith—the Award Distribution Center project team for precious insights and continued reinvention as the first real One-Page Project Managers took shape.

To the project teams that tackled: Cornerstone, Entrada, ISO 9000, Accounts Receivable, Shingo, and others for using and improving the One-Page Project Manager.

To Byron Terry, the genius behind the construction of every chart.

To Alan Horowitz for his invaluable work in putting my thoughts and ideas into the format of this book.

To Marjorie Campbell, Neal W. Hart, Dr. W. Dean Belnap, and O. Don Ostler for giving me projects that exceeded my grasp.

To Professor J. D. Seader a most remarkable teacher.

To Chester Elton and Adrian Gostick, best selling authors, for challenging and collegial counsel.

To John Wiley & Sons Senior Editor Laurie Harting for creativity, competence, encouragement, and wit.

Finally, to our children and grandchildren; the most challenging and rewarding projects of all.

A One-Page Project Manager: It May Seem like Magic— But It Is Very Real

Imagine. It is Friday afternoon; the president of your company just informed you that he has to report to the board of directors about your project and its status during their lunch break on Monday. He asks for a summary of your project, using text, graphs, and charts—including what aspects of it are on, ahead, or behind time; who is responsible for each of the project's major tasks; how the project is performing in terms of the budget; how well the project is meeting its objectives; what major problems have cropped up; and generally how well the project is presently progressing—coupled with a forecast for the next three months.

Providing all this information could fill a book. You consider calling up Microsoft Project, Primavera P3, or some other project management software program you have been diligently using and compiling all the requested data.

One thing holding you back is the time involved with preparing such a report. You and your team are deploying a major milestone this weekend, and a report like this will take up a lot of energy that would otherwise go to the project. The performance of the project could well suffer because your president wants such a comprehensive report.

In addition, you know that the board will, at best, be very limited on time. Senior managers usually only have the time to read highlights. They just cannot read all of a multipage report; instead, they look for key indicators and the most vital information. If this proves incomplete or unsatisfactory, they will be relentless in pursuit of understanding. Therefore, you must be thorough and disclose both good and bad news.

What do you do? Should you delay your deployment and devote all of the weekend and some of your best people to preparing such a report, or should you do the best you can, alone, and hope the board is diverted by other issues prior to their lunch, and therefore not as piercing as usual?

The best solution is actually neither of these. What you should do—and what you should have done from the beginning of your project—is simply provide a copy of your one-page project manager. It can be done quickly, easily, and without endangering the project's performance. All the information required can be summarized on one page using intuitive, meaningful graphics that even the busiest senior manager and board member will quickly comprehend.

That is the promise of the one-page project manager—it will convey all the salient information a project's stakeholders need to know and provide it in a timely, easy-to-understand, and easy-to-compile format. From my experience in managing dozens of projects— ranging from celebrating the bicentennial of the U.S. Constitution with Chief Justice Warren Berger, to implementing an SAP enterprisewide solution, to building an automated distribution center, to winning a coveted management prize, to reengineering a major business process, to launching a new Internet business, to gaining ISO 9000 certification—the one-page project manager works. It informs, keeps people focused on what is important, makes clear who is responsible for what, and tracks how well the project is performing based on several variables—all on one, simple, 8½-inch by 11-inch piece of paper.

Sound too good to be true? Is it magic or real? Read this book and you will see that every promise just made, the one-page project manager can fulfill.

1

Why This Book Is Needed

Project management is an academic discipline, a business activity, and a strategy—indeed, a profession. Some magazines and newsletters publish nothing but articles about it. A small library could be compiled consisting exclusively of books about it. There are training sessions, seminars, and certifications that focus on project management. Dozens of universities offer master's degrees in the discipline, and a few offer doctorates.

It might seem everything there is to know about project management already exists. With all the information available about the subject, it would be reasonable to assume that the only thing authors have to offer today is refinements to the discipline, a few insights, some tweaking here and there. Who really needs another book about project management?

I've been a project manager for over a quarter century. I've managed projects from those with budgets of a few thousand dollars and a handful of people to projects costing tens of millions of dollars and involving thousands of people.

CONCEPT No matter what the project—its goals or its purpose, large or small—certain aspects of managing a project are consistent. And one of these consistencies is the need to communicate.

Certainly, much has been written about communicating among the team members of a project. As I write this, I'm looking at a 1,000-plus-page textbook on project management, *Project Management,* ninth edition (New York: John Wiley & Sons, 2006, p. 234), by Harold Kerzner that notes: "Because of the time spent in a communications mode, the project manager may very well have as his or her responsibility the process of *communications management* [emphasis, the author's]. Communications management is the formal or informal process of conducting or supervising the exchange of information upward, downward, laterally, or diagonally. In short, the main business of project managers may be communication. There appears to be a direct correlation between the project manager's ability to manage the communications process and project performance."

This book is about project management communications, and therefore project performance. It is about straight talk that adequately and efficiently illustrates the whole story. But unlike anything I've ever seen written about project management communications, this book is primarily about communicating with those who are not part of the project, both inside and outside the organization. Yes, every project has an audience deeply interested in the project though not directly involved in it, yet few project managers know how to effectively communicate with this constituency.

This constituency includes the board of directors, senior management, suppliers, customers, superiors or subordinates indirectly involved with the project or its outcome, and others.

KEY CONCEPT Your success as a project manager is in direct proportion to your ability to communicate project performance (i.e., scope, timeliness, and planned versus actual resources), current completions, and future expectations.

The initial idea for this book, and more specifically the one-page project manager tool, came from a need I found in every project I managed—communicating a project's status, and the performance of those in charge of various aspects of the project, to the company's senior management.

Corporate management wants to know about projects, particularly larger ones. Even small projects have managers at some level in the corporate hierarchy who have an interest or responsibility for the project, yet are not directly part of the project. Bigger projects tend to attract the attention of more and more upper-level managers, with the biggest projects getting on the radar screen of the CEO and even the board of directors.

The founder of our company, Obert C. Tanner, was always intimately involved with all of our building projects, no matter how small or large. These were of great interest to him. However, computer software projects, even very large ones, he left to others from whom he expected simple reports of the complex project parameters.

Yet, these not-directly-involved managers, like Obert, don't want to spend a great deal of time studying the status of a project. If a supervisor on the project team isn't performing, management wants to know this, but doesn't want to spend time and effort ferreting out who is responsible. Whether a part of a project is running behind or is on time, or if a part is over budget, under budget, or on budget—these are things management wants to know. Management wants to know what's going on, who is performing well, who needs help, and what the overall status is of the project.

But—and this is important—they want to know this easily and quickly. Those not directly involved with a project but who have a vested interest in seeing it successfully completed, need to be communicated with in a way that engages them and doesn't waste their time. Long reports, detailed analyses of a project, and extended discussions of what's going on—well, those are almost certain to cause a manager's immediate attention to divert to other pressing issues.

KEY CONCEPT When asked to write a project status report, many project managers produce shallow or incomplete summaries in an attempt to make them short. Many such reports prompt more questions than they answer. In such cases, brevity breeds confusion. The one-page project manager answers more questions than it generates and is brief but sufficient, which is why it is such an effective communication tool.

Yet, when you read all that's written about project management, including all the articles and textbooks with hundreds and hundreds of pages, you'll find very little about how to communicate succinctly and effectively with supervisors who have an interest in a project but are not directly involved. There's lots written about what Kerzner called "communications management," but such discussions almost invariably involve how to communicate between members of the project team. Little is written about communicating to corporate management and even less about how to communicate in a way that accommodates management's need for brevity and ease of understanding.

The one-page project manager is a tool that was designed, from the beginning, as a way to engage upper management and make its job easier.

What Is the One-Page Project Manager?

I go into detail later about the makeup of the One-Page Project Manager (OPPM) and how to build one, but for now a simple definition is: The One-Page Project Manager is a tool or a report for senior management. This tool was created because we realized we needed to communicate to senior management about the status of a project beyond just simple comments, such as "we're on time and slightly under budget." We needed also to motivate and hold the owners of various tasks responsible for their work.

The One-Page Project Manager, using graphs and color, paints a highly visual, interlocking picture of a project. It links various parts and components, making immediately clear to senior management the status (in both time and cost) of all the major project components and who the owners of each component are. Because the names of all the responsible managers are on the document, motivation is created among these managers to perform. Outstanding performance that exceeds the plan shows up on this tool and senior management immediately sees who is personally responsible—and who deserves specific and timely recognition.

When an aspect of a project is going well, its line on the One-Page Project Manager is a bright green or a filled-in dot, so it is immediately visually apparent. When that aspect of the project is behind in terms of time or over in terms of budget, it is highlighted in bright red. When there is some ambiguity, it is highlighted in yellow.

Driving the development of the One-Page Project Manager was the acknowledgment that we at O.C. Tanner lacked, as a company, the discipline to consistently do a good job of managing projects. We just didn't have the skills needed to successfully manage projects on a consistent basis. The solution, we thought, was to send our managers to project management school, which we did. We also read many books and hired plenty of consultants—and got mired in project management planning and charting.

The minutia of projects—how many full-time-equivalent employees are needed, capacity utilization, the filling out of forms (we had 25 different forms), and so on—became the focus, and we got overwhelmed by the planning and bureaucracy. This affected our execution. This drive toward improved project management died of its own weight. We discovered that sometimes project planning becomes an end in itself and never ends.

The first One-Page Project Manager (see Figure 2.1) came about as a coagulation of ideas relating to organizing parts of a project around a simple matrix suggested by our president, Kent Murdock. Being a trial

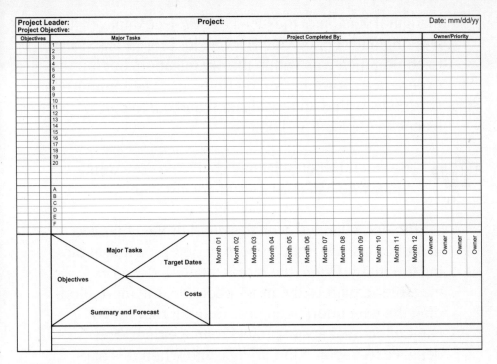

FIGURE 2.1 *The first One-Page Project Manager.*

Copyright O.C. Tanner 2007. **To customize this document, download it to your hard drive from the following web site: www.onepageprojectmanager.com.** The document can be opened, edited, and printed using Microsoft Excel or another popular spreadsheet application.

lawyer in a former life, Kent was used to simplifying complex issues into summaries sufficient to address the salient facts yet efficiently persuade a jury.

Our assignment was to replace a collection of disparate warehouses with a single, computer-automated storage-and-distribution center. A few project leaders sketched out the first One-Page Project Manager while sitting in an airport waiting for a delayed flight. Kent's suggested matrix provided the foundation on which we began creating a comprehensive and interlocking report document.

This effort led to a detailed discussion that continued after we returned home, eventually leading to the inaugural version of the One-Page Project Manager. It was originally conceived as a way for project managers to communicate *up* within the organization, but further experience showed it could also be used to communicate *down* within an organization and *out* to colleagues, suppliers, and others.

 Be careful when selecting your team. You want those who can execute and not just plan.

Efficient, effective, well-designed project management has just the right amount of details, while avoiding too many. Often, the more detailed, the more elegant the plan is, the more pedantic, the more plodding the execution becomes. To put it bluntly, you can be too anal about project management. The details can become the drivers, and when this happens, you lose sight of what's important and the management process becomes ineffective. Eventually, the project breaks down and fails. To use a cliché, you lose sight of the forest for the trees. Moreover, senior management does not need to, or want to, know all the details.

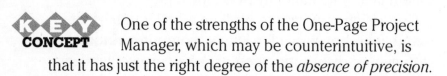 One of the strengths of the One-Page Project Manager, which may be counterintuitive, is that it has just the right degree of the *absence of precision*.

For example, the first project where we used this tool involved the building of a $10 million automated distribution center at our headquarters campus in Salt Lake City. There were computerized cranes being shipped from Japan to Salt Lake City, and whether they would arrive on time was a source of considerable concern.

Part of that concern was because of the distance involved, but part was a consequence of a devastating earthquake that had hit Kobe, Japan, on January 17, 1995, one month into the year-long project. The earthquake affected numerous distribution channels through which the crane components were arriving.

Management needed to know if this equipment would arrive on time, if this process was on budget, and who was responsible for making sure this happened, but it didn't need to know the details of how the cranes made their way to Salt Lake City from Japan, and all the effort that had to be expended to make sure the right equipment arrived at the right time.

 The One-Page Project Manager navigates between failing to plan and overplanning. The plan is just the beginning—the means to the end, but not the end.

The One-Page Project Manager showed management how the crane aspect of this project was progressing, but not every detail behind this part of the project. The One-Page Project Manager was able to give senior management detailed, but not overly detailed, information and present this information in a quick, easily understood, easily digestible format. Project task owners know and manage the details—senior management doesn't need to, or want to, know these details. These owners also know that management is watching their performance.

 The One-Page Project Manager makes all of a project's owners readily identifiable to everyone. Owners have no place to hide when a project is being monitored with a One-Page Project Manager.

The One-Page Project Manager makes clear—visually, through the use of interconnected graphics and color— who is responsible for what and how they are performing. Senior management sees, immediately by glancing at one page, who is performing well and who is behind on their portion of the project.

Not only does this visualization make it easier for management to understand a project's status and who is responsible, but it also is an important motivator to the owners. They know that their role and performance is continually and immediately visible to senior management.

CONCEPT

The One-Page Project Manager is a tool that can be used in a surprisingly wide array of projects.

Its first use was for a construction project, but at O.C. Tanner, we've also used it for:

- *Implementation of a software project.* An enterprise-resource-planning (ERP) project using SAP software that cost $30 million.
- *Launching a new Internet business.* Entrada, which provides performance awards that companies give to their top-performing employees.
- *Obtaining ISO 9000 certification.*
- *Addressing a long-standing problem.* An accounts-receivable reduction project that reduced accounts receivable almost a full month.
- *Winning a prize.* The Shingo Prize, which is an award that is given for excellence in manufacturing. O.C. Tanner won it in 1999.

The One-Page Project Manager we have today evolved through several years and a number of projects to the tool that we now use.

The One-Page Project Manager clarifies your thinking and can provide unexpected benefits. For example, in our project to reduce accounts receivable, the One-Page Project Manager revealed that of the four processes involved with accounts receivables, the process of generating invoices had no owner. As a result, it was out of control. The One-Page Project Manager made clear there was a problem here. Knowing this, we were quickly able to assign an owner to this part of the process, the process was brought under control, and the entire accounts-receivable process was improved.

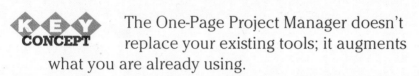 The One-Page Project Manager doesn't replace your existing tools; it augments what you are already using.

The information presented isn't new. What's new is that existing information is placed in a format that is easy to use and to read. That's not a trivial distinction. By placing information in a new, easy-to-grasp format, management becomes better informed and those involved with the project become more highly motivated.

An argument could be made that the success of projects is enhanced and improved through the use of the One-Page Project Manager.

Project Overview

WHAT IS A PROJECT?

Before we can discuss the One-Page Project Manager, we need to define project management. I don't think my definition of project management is unusual, but it helps if we all start from the same place with the same view of the topic under consideration.

I view projects as activities with well-defined parameters, with their own time frames and goals. They are outside the course of a job's or a company's everyday activities. They are something a bit different, a bit special. They go beyond the ordinary.

And they are not repeated. Ordinary work, such as writing scheduled reports, dealing with customer questions, and studying financial statements, are all repeated over and over again. This is not true for projects. Projects have defined goals, and a beginning, a middle, and an end. In Chapter 1, I listed some of the projects that have used the One-Page Project Manager. Obtaining ISO 9000 certification, for example,

project. Perhaps there will be another
at we'll want, but the ISO 9000 project
had its own goal and timetable, and
dinary for us. The same can be said of
uilding we constructed and the ERP
entation project, as well as numerous
...er projects.

Furthermore, a project has resources (e.g., people, money, equipment) assigned specifically to it. These resources are outside the resources used to operate the business.

Projects also create something that did not exist before. We had a new distribution center after we built our distribution building: The building didn't exist prior to the completion of the project. Entrada was a new business for us that hadn't existed previously.

Manufacturing recognition awards for our customers is an ongoing activity, our core business, without any beginning and end, and as such is not a project. Consider:

- Maintaining the distribution building isn't a project, but building the building is.
- Keeping up our ISO 9000 certification isn't a project, but getting the certification in the first place is.
- Using our Enterprise-Resource-Planning (ERP) software isn't a project, but installing it is.

Here is how Paula Martin and Karen Tate, in their book, *Project Management Memory Jogger* (Salem, NH: Goal/QPC, 1997) define a project:

A project is any temporary, organized effort that creates a unique product, service, process, or plan. It can be as simple as the plan for an off-site retreat or as complex as the construction of a medical center, with a team size ranging from a few people or hundreds or even thousands who are working in one location or across continents.

Projects bring together people from a range of jobs and provide them with the opportunity to collaborate in a unique way. (p. 1)

WHAT IS PROJECT MANAGEMENT?

Now that we have an idea of what a project is, we can consider what project management is. Here is Kerzner's definition from *Project Management* (New York: John Wiley & Sons, 2006):

Project management is the planning, organizing, directing, and controlling of company resources for a relatively short-term objective that has been established to complete specific goals and objectives. Furthermore, project management utilizes the systems approach to management by having functional personnel (the vertical hierarchy) assigned to a specific project (the horizontal hierarchy). (p. 4)

Martin and Tate give this definition:

Project management supplies project teams with a process that helps them coordinate their efforts so they may create the right product (or service, process or plan), at the right time, for the right customer, within the resource limits established by the organization. (p. 2)

17

I think both these definitions are very helpful. They address critical issues such as teams, planning, organizing, resources, coordination, systems, and goals. All of these are essential elements of a project, and project management brings a coordinated approach to these with a goal in mind.

BENEFITS OF PROJECT MANAGEMENT

The One-Page Project Manager is a tool used as part of the much larger discipline of project management. The driving force behind improving the project management skills of an organization is the realization that many projects have been poorly managed— usually to the detriment of the organization (wasted time and money, lost opportunities, loss of competitive strength). Sometimes, poorly managed projects have had devastating effects on their organizations. Not long ago, we had two major competitors. All of us implemented ERP systems; only O.C. Tanner did it successfully (though not without considerable delays and challenges). Because of the costs and disruptions to their businesses from their failed ERP projects, one gave up and retreated to legacy systems, while the other was forced to "go live" too soon. Both firms were eventually sold and no longer operate as they did in the past. Both were devastated—fatally wounded, in fact—by their failed projects.

KEY CONCEPT Good project management can be the difference not just between a successful project versus an unsuccessful one, but the difference between a successful business and a failed one.

Implementing a comprehensive approach to managing projects creates a number of benefits. Effective management improves the chances that a project will be successful, on budget, on time, done right, and done efficiently. Mistakes are likely to be caught earlier and therefore dealt with faster and more efficiently than if they had been allowed to go on. Resources are likely to be used more effectively. Wasted money is kept to a minimum, thus improving profitability.

Control of a project improves project management skills. *Scope creep,* the subtle, unintended enlargement of a project (which often has destructive consequences on the budget, the people involved, and the project's time frame), can be held in check with strong project management.

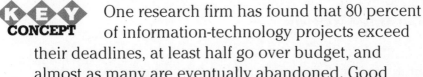 One research firm has found that 80 percent of information-technology projects exceed their deadlines, at least half go over budget, and almost as many are eventually abandoned. Good project management can avoid such disasters.

Project management can deal with a great majority of problems that need to be solved. For example, O.C. Tanner manufactures and distributes millions of recognition awards each year. We had to match the corporate emblems that are affixed to awards (these are often made of gold and diamonds) to the awards themselves (e.g., pens, clocks, watches), affixing them, wrapping them, and getting them back out to delivery trucks efficiently. That was our problem. Our solution: Build a centralized distribution center. The role of project management was to make that distribution warehouse a reality. We got it built on time, under budget, and delivered a return on investment well in excess of our promise. The bottom line: We are far more efficient than we have ever been before. Project management as a discipline helped us achieve this.

ASPECTS OF EFFECTIVE PROJECT MANAGEMENT

This isn't a book about how to manage a project in its entirety, but it is worth discussing some basic techniques that can help make your project management skills more effective. By knowing basic project management skills, you will be able to use the One-Page Project Manager more effectively.

Communication

Communication is perhaps the most important aspect of managing any project. Project leaders must communicate. Regular team meetings, e-mails, one-on-one meetings, reports, and the like must be integral parts of every project. The ultimate responsibility for communication rests with the project leader. And the One-Page Project Manager becomes a vital communication tool.

Team Orientation

Projects typically cross department lines. Marketing, customer service, information technology, and finance, for example, might all be involved in a help-desk project. Every affected department must be involved with planning the project and in helping to make it a success. The project needs the buy-in of those affected.

Initiative Taking

When you own part of a project, you can't assume the role of victim, even though you may indeed be subject to someone else's performance (or nonperformance). You have to take the initiative to make things happen.

We call this the "French bread principle." Typically, task owners tend to look at a project like a loaf of Wonder Bread, sliced in vertical pieces, each piece neatly individualized, self-contained, and dependent on the previous slice. They sit comfortably (and justifiably) waiting for the completion of some previous task over which they have no responsibility. This doesn't work. Owners need to slice diagonally through the project like French bread, assisting other owners on whose performance they depend.

Don't wait for someone else to get things done. If things aren't getting done, take personal responsibility to help. As noted, good project management is team oriented. If a player on a basketball team is having a poor shooting night, his or her teammates don't point a finger at their struggling teammate and say, "Hey, I'm covering my man (or woman)." They have to step up and do the scoring. That's teamwork, and it applies to project management as well as sports.

One Leader

Ultimately, like a car, there has to be one person in the driver's seat, one go-to manager. Projects typically do not lend themselves to management by committee.

A project leader must first provide the vision, the "burning platform." This project mission and objective must be clear and exciting—as we say, "it must be worth it." Second, the leader secures alignment of the project team and management to do the mission of the project. This is the hard part. The leader then, in cooperation with the team, establishes the expectations and owners necessary to accomplish the mission. Finally, a leader must build trust and frequently recognize people for their outstanding performance.

Five Essential Parts of a Project—And the One-Page Project Manager

Elements

- *Tasks:* The how
- *Objectives:* The what and the why
- *Timeline:* The when
- *Cost:* The how much
- *Owners:* The who

Every project has five essential elements. It is not coincidental that the One-Page Project Manager also has the same five elements; we have used the elements that make up projects as the structure on which we built the One-Page Project Manager (see Figure 4.1). The five elements are:

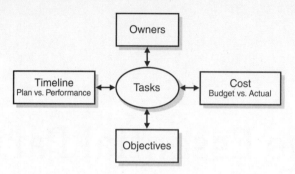

FIGURE 4.1 *Five essential elements for every project.*

1. *Tasks: The how*—Tasks are the center of a project and need to be done to accomplish the objectives. They are not about making people feel good, rather they are about the nuts and bolts of a project—the specifics of what needs to be done.

2. *Objectives: The what and the why*—The purpose of a project is its vision. Ken Blanchard, in his book, *The Heart of a Leader* (Tulsa, OK: Eagle Publishing, 2002) writes, "Knowing where you are going is the first step in getting there." A project's objectives can be general or specific but are always measured by whether they are done on time and on budget. If desired, more aspects to objectives may be added, such as return on investment (ROI).

3. *Timeline: The when*—When things are supposed to be done (and when they are actually done) are monitored on the timeline. If you expand a project, you have to expand the time and the money allotted. "Time is a versatile performer. It flies, marches on, heals all wounds, runs out, and will tell," writes Franklin P. Jones, as quoted in *Wise*

Words and Quotes (Colorado Springs, CO: Tyndale House, 2000) by Vernon McLellan.

4. *Cost: The how much*—Some costs are capitalized, such as building materials, requiring cash now and affecting income through future depreciation. Project expenses can have *hard* costs, like consulting, or *soft* costs, as with internal staff deployed on the project. Cost accounting can be complicated and every project needs input from accounting professionals.

5. *Owners: The who*—It's hard to overemphasize the importance of ownership. If *you* know what tasks you own, you know *management* knows. And if management knows, management is watching; and if management is watching, you are definitely engaged.

 The One-Page Project Manager gets people who are involved in the project to think and act like owners.

The One-Page Project Manager makes the name of every project's owner public for all to see, including senior management. It engages those involved in a project. As they see how their part of a project is progressing, they know that others see how well they are performing: Ownership is a key to engagement.

Full engagement requires both heart and mind:

- *Heart:* An understanding and commitment to a project's vision, complete with a clear understanding about what you own, engages the heart. Documentation and display of your ownership magnifies this understanding and commitment. When the owner knows that colleagues, senior management, or others know about this ownership, the owner's emotional engagement with a project deepens.

- *Mind:* The One-Page Project Manager provides a clear connection between ownership and the project's objectives and metrics. The mind portion of project management involves showing what the participants own and how the objectives are measured.

Clear ownership illuminates the winners and losers, namely those who deserve to be recognized and receive commendations for jobs well done and those who need to be assisted. The One-Page Project Manager makes it easier to be sure that everyone who deserves recognition receives it because all the major owners of a project are listed on the tool. This isn't trivial because acknowledgment and rewards are proven motivators. Yet, senior management often doesn't know who to reward or appreciate. They often get their information from sound bites—comments from managers or others, things they hear, or feelings they have about a person or a piece of the project. This can cause over rewarding the undeserving or underappreciating those who perform well.

 With the One-Page Project Manager, responsible owners are clearly manifest.

OWNERSHIP IS REMARKABLY POWERFUL

The following five cases exemplify how ownership generates engagement, and often some unexpected accomplishments.

Shingo Prize Project

We had one month to submit our application for the Shingo Prize. Senior management didn't think we could do it. I invited anyone in the company who wanted to help, to join the team. They would not earn any extra money, and the work would be done after hours. The team, in fact, worked from 5:00 P.M. to midnight for a month to complete this project. They understood the vision, were energized by the thought of beating the odds, and were welded together by a single, time-constrained focus. It was an energized team; it created a very emotional and productive climate. You can keep a team on that level of commitment for only a short time. We did it for one month, and we succeeded and brought home the prize—literally and metaphorically.

Boiler Stack

As we were building an automated distribution center, we discovered late in the project that the boiler stack was required by building codes to extend five feet above the building. This would mean an ugly, tall, wired-down, galvanized stack rising above our beautiful building. To reroute it would cost $100,000, which wasn't in the budget. The owner of that part of the project took it on himself to find a solution. He ferreted out an obscure opportunity. If a blower was installed in the stack, the code said the stack didn't have to extend beyond the roofline and, with a little paint; he could almost hide this unplanned distraction. For $10,000, a workable solution involving a blower was found. This employee had a personal, emotional connection because he had a great deal of ownership in this project. This ownership came about because his name was on the One-Page Project Manager connected to this part of the project—and the objective to complete the project within budget.

ISO 9000

This project demonstrates an aspect of ownership not often thought about. We hired consultants to help us get this coveted international certification. When consultants are brought in, it's easy to dump responsibility and blame on them. We find that doesn't work well in project management. For that reason, *every owner on a One-Page Project Manager has to be our employee.* Consultants and other outsiders are not principle owners. This project was successfully completed in five months rather then the expected six, in part because a highly motivated, energized O.C. Tanner leader owned each piece, not the consultants.

Accounts Receivable Project

For years, our accounts receivable were too high. Previous attempts to resolve this problem would push responsibility down to the collections department. We set up a formal project, complete with a One-Page Project Manager, and on that tool, we placed the names of *sales* vice presidents. After all, it was the sales department that was generating all these accounts receivable, and a sale really isn't a sale until the money is collected. This got the attention of the right people and, once they took ownership, major changes occurred. This, combined with assigning an owner to the set-up, invoicing, and collecting processes resulted in a reduction of unpaid accounts by 25 days.

ERP Project

Lest you think that the One-Page Project Manager is a cure-all, a guarantee that all projects will be highly successful, there's the ERP project we did at O.C. Tanner. We delivered it on budget, and it had the return on investment promised, but it was not delivered on time. Actually, it took more than twice as long as originally forecast. However, management was able to accommodate this schedule because it knew, as the project progressed, why the project was running late and by how much. It knew this because every two weeks it received an updated One-Page Project Manager that clearly showed which aspects of the project were falling behind the desired timeline and which were on time. The One-Page Project Manager could not, by itself, bring this project in on time, but it could communicate to management what was happening, where the difficulties were, who was responsible, and what to expect.

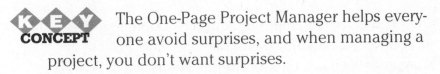 The One-Page Project Manager helps everyone avoid surprises, and when managing a project, you don't want surprises.

Let's now look at the One-Page Project Manager in Figure 4.2.

THE MATRIX

In Figure 4.2, toward the bottom, left-hand corner, a rectangle is divided into five, unequal, pie-like pieces. This rectangle represents the heart of the One-Page Project Manager. We call it the *Matrix*—the point where all the elements of the One-Page Project Manager—

Project Leader: Clark Campbell
Project Objective: Reengineer Distribution—30% ROI
Project: Automated Distribution Center (ADC)
Date: 12/01/94

Objectives	Major Tasks	Project Completed By: December 31, 1995	Owner/Priority
O	1 Award Contracts	O O	A
O	2 Site Demolition	O O	A B
O	3 System Software Design	O O O O	B A B
O	4 Computer Hardware Specifications	O O O	A
O	5 Workstation Design	O O O O O	B C A
O	6 Parking and Landscape	O O O O	A B
O	7 Footings and Foundations	O O O O O O	A
O	8 Columns and Beams	O O O	A
O	9 Roof Cap	O O	A
O	10 Main Floor Finish	O O O O	A C B
O	11 Exterior and Glass	O O O O O	A B
O	12 Computer Hardware Installed	O O	B A C
O O	13 Rack Installed	O O	B A B
O O	14 Automated Cranes Installed	O O	B A B B
O O	15 Conveyors Installed	O O	B A B B
O	16 Software Designed and Installed	O O O O O O O O	B A B
O	17 User Training	O O O O	A C B
O	18 Mezzanine Floor Finish	O O O O	A B B
O	19 Work Station and Furniture	O O O O O O O O O	B B A
O	20 Worker Transition	O	B A
O	21 Inventory Transfer	O O	A B B
O	22 Staffing	O O O O O	B A
O	A Internal Software Operational		A B
O	B External Software Operational		B A
O	C Integration Software Operational		B A B
O O O	D Full Consolidation Operational		B A B
O O O	E Go Live on Time		A A A A

Major Tasks / Target Dates / Objectives / Costs / Summary and Forecast

Months: Jan-95, Feb-95, Mar-95, Apr-95, May-95, Jun-95, Jul-95, Aug-95, Sep-95, Oct-95, Nov-95, Dec-95

Owners: Dennis, Wayne, Klaus, Dave

Building Complete / Systems Operational / People Deployed

Building $6.0 million
System $3.0 million
People $0.5 million

The ADC Project is scheduled to start January 1, 1995 and be completed by December 31, 1995. It will cost $10 million and will deliver an initial ROI of 30%.

FIGURE 4.2 *The One-Page Project Manager.*

and project management in general—come together. As you become familiar with the One-Page Project Manager, you'll see that its various elements all flow to this rectangle.

I introduce each part of the One-Page Project Manager in this chapter and go into more detail in later chapters.

Tasks

In the top part of the Matrix is a triangle labeled *Major Tasks.* Above that is a column listing the project's major tasks. How many tasks you list depends on the project and how detailed you want to be. But be aware that too many tasks will minimize the effectiveness of the One-Page Project Manager. It could become clumsy and overwhelming. Plus, you have only one page for everything. Include too many tasks, and you won't fit everything on the one page.

In the example shown here, we have room for 30 major project tasks. Even for very large projects, this is usually enough. With smaller projects, show fewer tasks. Shortly, I'll walk you through the building of an actual One-Page Project Manager and you'll see how the task portion of the tool is developed.

Keep in mind that behind each of these tasks, you could have another One-Page Project Manager or Microsoft Project or P3 Program Evaluation and Review Technique (PERT) charts. Let's say you are constructing a building and the One-Page Project Manager with the topmost view, the one seen by highest management, has as a major task the construction of the foundation. On one line of the form, you could write, "constructing foundation." That task could then have its own One-Page Project Manager that covers the major tasks involved with constructing the foundation, such as digging the hole, constructing supports, and pouring the concrete. And each of these could have its own One-Page Project Manager, and so forth. Also, *Subjective Tasks* (lines A through E) are for reporting qualitative performance. More is said about this in a later chapter.

KEY CONCEPT Projects are all about getting things done, about turning activities into results. Ultimately, projects are not about *activities*, but about successfully completing *tasks*.

Tasks are really the centerpiece of any project—the heart of the One-Page Project Manager. Constructing a building involves many different tasks, and ideally, they are done correctly, on time and on budget.

Target Dates

Moving clockwise around the Matrix, we next come to the section labeled *Target Dates*—the dates the tasks are to be completed, and the intermediary dates for each step that needs to be completed before the entire task is done. This section provides the timeline for each task.

Budget versus Cost

We use a simple bar chart in the open box to the right of the cost triangle. Usually two bars extend across the page, one for the capital budget and one for the expense budget. Costs are plotted as the project progresses.

Summary and Forecast

Write notes about aspects of the project not covered by the other sectors of the One-Page Project Manager in the *Summary*.

The space available for the Summary is limited. That's by design. It forces the project manager to think and write succinctly. Brevity communicates. Never reiterate in the Summary and Forecast what is already illustrated on the One-Page

Project Manager. Focus on explaining deviations from plan, together with a forecast of remedies. Knowing what you now know, give management your newly informed view of how the project will appear by the completion of the next two or three time boxes.

Objectives

Objectives need to be measurable and verifiable. They are the desired results of the project, and, as you can see on the One-Page Project Manager, objectives are tied to the various tasks. Not every objective is tied to every task.

For example, a construction project might have as its objectives for each task: Building Complete, Systems Operational, and People Deployed. One task would be: Columns and beams erected. That could be tied to the objective of Building Complete. Another task could be the installation of certain software. The objective tied to this would be System Operational. The task of software user training is tied to People Deployed.

5

Twelve Steps to Constructing the One-Page Project Manager

Let's now get started on how to *construct* a One-Page Project Manager. I've broken down the process into 12 bite-sized pieces that can be altered and changed to meet whatever project you are working on:

1. Header
2. Owners
3. Matrix
4. Project objectives
5. Major project tasks
6. Aligning tasks with objectives
7. Target dates
8. Aligning tasks to timeline
9. Aligning tasks to owners
10. Subjective tasks

11. Costs

12. Summary and forecast

Each portion of the tool is illustrated at least twice—blank and filled in. In the text, you will find a reduced copy of the form, but at the end of the chapter, full-page copies of the forms illustrate the progression you follow in building the One-Page Project Manager.

The filled in illustrations are from the project we called Automated Distribution Center. We at O.C. Tanner are in the business of creating and distributing various types of employee awards—recognition, performance, safety, and other types.

The Automated Distribution Center (ADC) is a building we constructed in 1995 that is dominated by a section filled with 30-foot-high shelving where our inventory of awards is stored (Figure 5.1). Found between the rows are shelves with robotic carriers that run on tracks and can pick out one award at a time out of the tens of thousands of awards we inventory at any given moment. They can restock the shelves as well. The stocking and retrieving of our awards inventory is entirely automatic.

CONSTRUCTING AND FILLING IN THE ONE-PAGE PROJECT MANAGER

The team leader and the project's owners fill in the One-Page Project Manager. They build it, and then they live with it.

 The One-Page Project Manager must be a team effort; your team consists of all the task

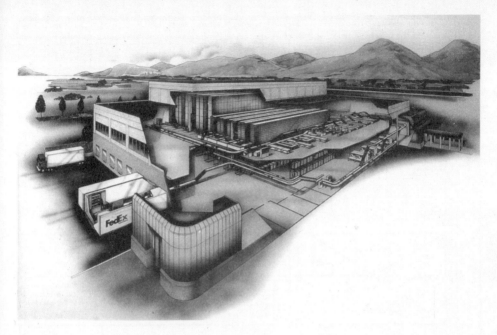

FIGURE 5.1   *The Automated Distribution Center.*

owners. You may have to negotiate with team members but, ultimately, you need buy-in and consensus from your team.

Now let's create a One-Page Project Manager.

STEP 1: THE HEADER

What It Is

The first step is to provide basic information about the project. This goes at the top of the form in the highlighted rectangle (Figure 5.2).
This information includes:

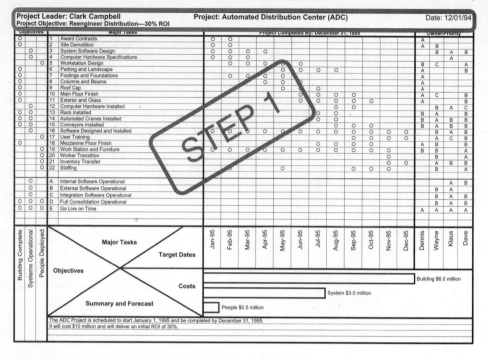

FIGURE 5.2   *The One-Page Project Manager—Step 1.*

- Project name
- Project leader
- Project objective
- Project completion date

How to Do It

Project Name: Automated Distribution Center

In our example, the name given the project is purely descriptive—Automated Distribution Center. Naming the project sounds simple, and to some degree it is. But don't take this task lightly. The name you give will be in front of everyone involved with the project every day, as well as those looking at the project (such as senior management). For this reason, having the objective of the project be part of the name is often a good idea. Examples: Reducing Accounts Receivable Project—not Reengineering Project #2; Winning Shingo Prize Project—not Manufacturing Excellence Award. Using the name to subtly reinforce the purpose of the project to participants day after day has value.

When naming the project, recognize the power of language. *Apollo Project,* the United States' project to reach the moon, made for a great sound bite, which is why it was such an effective project name. *The Titanic Project,* on the other hand, would probably send the wrong message. Don't get too cute with a project's name, but a catchy title can help engage people and have the project stand out among many projects.

You might want to hold off naming the project until you have your team in place. Then, together, everyone can contribute to the project's name.

Project Leader: Clark Campbell

I was assigned by senior management to lead this project. Each project must, ultimately, have one owner, one project leader. This person's name is the one that goes at the top of the One-Page Project Manager. Everyone who reads the form knows who is ultimately in charge of and responsible for the project.

In Step 1, the executive in charge must be identified. Let me be clear: This person must be the one in charge. This cannot be an advisor, a consultant, or anyone who is not a full-time employee of your organization.

We won't go into great detail about the abilities needed by the project manager, but since we are addressing the issue of communication, we should be clear that this manager has to be an excellent communicator.

I've divided the communications skills needed by project managers into three types:

- *Up:* This is communication that goes from the person up the hierarchy to upper levels of supervision and management.
- *Down:* This is communication that goes from the person down the hierarchy to subordinates.
- *Out:* This is communication that goes from the person out to his or her associates, colleagues, and peers. In the organization's hierarchy, these are folks at the same level as the project manager.

Most people are not equally adept at all forms of communication. Some are very competent and comfortable in the president's office; they are good at up communication. Others work well with their peers, but are disasters when dealing with the board of directors. Still others are good at motivating those below them, but don't know how to communicate well with supervisors, nor interact well with peers.

Every project manager needs to be good at what I call "straight talk." This is talk that is honest, complete, to the point, and addresses issues that you might otherwise not wish to discuss. If your project is in trouble, you need to say so, not cover it up. If you're a bit worried, that too needs to be conveyed. Straight talk is not pessimism. It is honesty. If a piece of a project is behind schedule and other parts of the project are thereby being held up, the straight-talking project manager will acknowledge the problem, be honest about its consequences, and then devise a strategy that lets the project team continue where it can be productive, while assisting the behind-schedule part of the project to catch up. This is honest optimism—it is saying, "We can do this and that and help the project along" while acknowledging the problems and challenges.

TIP Never hide critical issues from management or your team. Why? (1) No one likes surprises; (2) the help and support you get from others when they learn of your problems may pleasantly surprise you.

Here's an example of straight talk—and the lack thereof. I don't know if this story is true or apocryphal, but it doesn't matter. The message it sends is certainly accurate. Someone was planning a very large breakfast meeting and was talking to the caterer to see if the meeting was feasible, given certain requirements. The meeting planner asked if it would be possible to have the meeting at 6:00 A.M. The caterer immediately said, "No problem." Next question: We will have 500 people. Is that a problem? The immediate response: No problem. Next question: We want to serve everyone an 8-ounce glass of orange juice. Is that a problem? The immediate response: No problem. The next question: We want this orange juice to be freshly squeezed. Is that a problem? The immediate response: No problem. That's when the event planner knew he was in trouble. Squeezing 500 8-ounce glasses of orange juice to be ready at 6:00

A.M. is a definite challenge. The caterer wasn't giving the event planner straight talk. He was shining over the challenges, hoping to win the business. A variation on this would be if the caterer had started complaining about squeezing all this fresh orange juice early in the morning and saying it couldn't be done. That's not straight talk either—that's a naysayer who is a pessimist and unwilling to serve his clients.

What would a straight talker say? When asked if it was possible to serve 500 8-ounce glasses of fresh squeezed orange juice first thing in the morning, he would say, "Let me think about that," take out his calculator, figure out how much orange juice was needed, how many oranges would have to be ordered and stored, and how many machines and people it would take to produce the desired amount of orange juice at the prescribed time. Then he would calculate the costs and quote a price. This is straight talk. It's not trying to avoid a situation or gloss over it. Instead, it is trying to meet the challenge in an honest and productive way. Project managers should always engage in straight talk.

I'm going into this detail about communication because, ultimately, the One-Page Project Manager is a communication tool. As I have already noted, it was first designed to communicate to upper management—up communication. But over time we have found it effective at communicating *out* with those in the organization who have a stake in the project, and *down* to those working on the project.

Project Objective: Reengineer Distribution ROI—30%

The project's objective is usually given to the project manager by the same people who gave him or her the project in the first place. If, as project manager, you are not given the project's objective, go back to those who gave you the project and get it. They need to know the project's objective. If they don't, you, they, and the project will all be in trouble. If they are unclear about the project's objective, here are a couple of questions to ask them that will help them focus on what the project is all about:

- Why do you want the project to be done?
- What do you hope to gain from the project?

When you have the project's objective, write it down. This allows everyone to see it and to make sure everyone is in agreement. The objective of any project is the project's purpose, what you want to do, what you want to accomplish. "Gaining ISO 9000 Certification" could be both the name of a project and the objective of a project. Typically, the objective would be aimed at:

- Creating . . .
- Completing . . .
- Implementing . . .

You need to write down the project's objective in just a few words. It should not be a paragraph, but rather a sentence or fragment of a sentence.

Defining the project's objective is not something you, the executive in charge of the project, can do in isolation. This is not something that should come from on high and be forced on those involved. The objective needs to be worked out by the stakeholders. These include the team who will work on the project, senior management, which is providing funding for the project, and anyone else who will benefit from the project. If you don't involve the various stakeholders, there's a good chance you will try to achieve something the stakeholders don't want—or won't accept because they had no say in the project's objective.

In our example, we really had two high-level objectives. One was to reengineer distribution. We have thousands and thousands of awards in inventory at any one time, and as the business grew, efficiently inventorying them, tracking them, and retrieving them became increasingly difficult. As a result, we decided to start from a clean slate and build a place designed to provide the most efficient, the most automated distribution that we could.

The ultimate purpose, of course, was to save money, which relates to the second part of the objective—ROI (return on investment) of 30 percent. This project, which cost nearly $10 million, had as its objective an ROI of 30 percent a year. This meant it would have to save the company about $3 million (or 30 percent of $10 million) a year. Where did this figure of having an ROI of 30 percent come from? From upper management. This project needed to produce an ROI of 30 percent to be financially justifiable. Note that this figure was placed right at the top of the One-Page Project Manager because it was a major objective and everyone involved had to keep it in mind throughout the project.

Project Completion Date: 12/31/95

Like the objective, those who give you the project usually set the completion or target date. *Do not take this date lightly*. This is a very important date because your performance and that of your team will be judged, to a great degree, by how well you meet this date. Though the powers that be may give you a date, that doesn't mean you have to blindly accept it. You and your team must study the project and decide on whether the date you are given (assuming you are given a date, which is likely) is realistic. If not, you need to make clear *before* you place the date on the One-Page Project Manager that the proposed date needs to be changed. Maybe you won't be able to change it, but you need to try if you think it is unrealistic. Do not start the project and, six months later, start complaining to upper management that the completion date can't be met. By then it's too late. You are much better off negotiating at the beginning for a new date. Once you put the completion date on the One-Page Project Manager, it is, essentially, carved in stone and you are stuck with it.

If management's date remains unrealistic to you during the initial completion of the header, simply indicate that after you have selected your project team, together you will craft a plan that would increase the probability of delivering the objective. This could very well mean upward adjustments in people or costs, or downward adjustment in the scope of deliverables.

Step 1 blank appears on page 85 and Step 1 completed appears on page 86.

STEP 2: THE OWNERS
What It Is

We'll assume from this point on you are the project's executive, because this is the person who typically puts the One-Page Project Manager together (of course, with the help of the others on the project team). Your next step is to name your team. Who will be on it? Who will be working on the project? Who will be responsible for the parts of the project? These are the people who will manage the major components of the project and will be instrumental to your success in managing the project. In Figure 5.3, the highlighted box along the right side has space for the names of the owners. Here is where you place the names of those on your immediate team. In the form on page 66 that's filled out, the owners are listed as Dennis, Wayne, Klaus, and Dave.

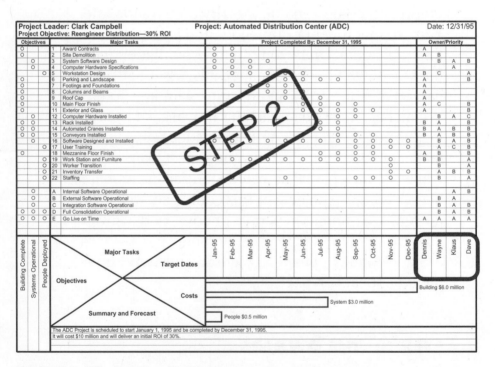

FIGURE 5.3   *The One-Page Project Manager—Step 2.*

How to Do It

Some pointers on how to name your team, indeed your "owners." Of course, you must match people with the needs and requirements of the project. You'll have to consider each person's experience, knowledge, and skills—and how they fit the project's needs. And you should also consider personalities. How well do these people work together? If two people, for instance, are known to dislike one another, it doesn't mean they both cannot be on the team. It just means, if you put them both on the team, you think you can manage their differences and that the extra work of managing them is worth the benefits each brings to the overall project.

Also, keep the number of owners as small as possible. From my experience, three or four is usually about right. On a large project, you'll have more than one layer of one-page project managers, and each of these will have its own set of owners. Each One-Page Project Manager should be limited to a handful of owners.

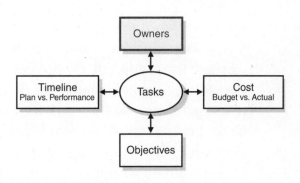

Let me say a few more words about the owners. The success of your project largely depends on them. If they're good, if they're engaged, if they're effective, if they can execute and make things happen, chances are very high your project will be a success.

This is critical: Your owners must be able to execute, to make things happen. If they can't, find new owners.

You, as the lead manager, must also know the amount of time your owners can contribute to the project. Are they working on it full-time? If so, does their home department expect them to continue to do some of their original job function? When this happens, you have a potential problem, because these people are working more than one full-time job. If a person is supposed to work for your project one-quarter time, but his or her home department hasn't reduced any of the person's responsibilities during the life of the project, you face the same type of problem.

That said, recognize that often the people involved with a project, especially a project that has generated a strong commitment from its owners and participants, will find the time the project needs. They'll find a way to get the job done even though, as project owners, they typically do not get any additional compensation or relief from some of their nonproject responsibilities for the work they do on the project. Note, getting part of an employee's time who is a winner, can be more valuable than getting all of the time of a employee who is a moderate performer. Keep this in mind when choosing your team.

Also, as a group, you'd do well to have the owners represent a variety of viewpoints, and not just view things similarly between them. You might want a realist, a skeptic, and a Pollyanna-type person. Each has strengths and weaknesses, but together, they can make a formidable team, able to handle a variety of obstacles and challenges.

STEP 3: THE MATRIX—THE TOOL'S FOUNDATION

What It Is

Earlier I talked about the Matrix. Think of this as the hub, the focal point, and the intersection where all points meet. Or, to use another metaphor, think of it as a compass that will guide your project from start to finish. As you'll see on the next illustration, this is the step where you construct the Matrix while in conversation with your team. The Matrix provides the foundation for the entire One-Page Project Manager and links all of a project's essential elements. It communicates these elements to your readers (Figure 5.4).

How to Do It

What you will do in this step is gather your team and start the discussion of how to handle this project. You'll present an overview of the project to your team, and in rough outline, discuss the pieces of the Matrix, including objectives, major project tasks, target dates, and budget. Admittedly, the Matrix, and the One-Page Project Manager, in general, is a rather simplified way of looking at a project. But that's one of the strengths of the One-Page Project Manager—it does not try to do everything involved with a project. It just takes the pieces of information of most interest and value to upper management and others, and presents them in a format that's quickly and easily followed and understood. That's its strength, and the Matrix is where all the important steps of the One-Page Project Manager converge.

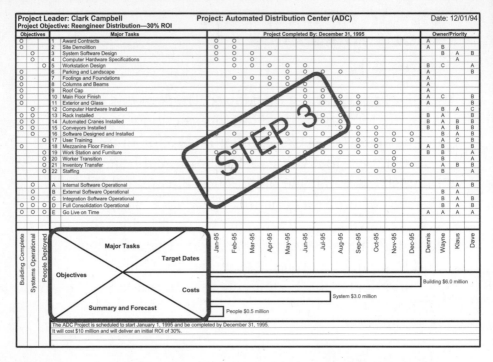

FIGURE 5.4   *The One-Page Project Manager—Step 3.*

Copyright O.C. Tanner 2007. **To customize this document, download it to your hard drive from the following web site: www.onepageprojectmanager.com.** The document can be opened, edited, and printed using Microsoft Excel or another popular spreadsheet application.

During Step 3, the project manager tutors each team member on how to build and use the One-Page Project Manager. You will find that as you and your staff struggle through completing the 12 steps—a team will come together. You will experience a growing competence and confidence in your joint ability to successfully complete your assigned project—together.

STEP 4: PROJECT OBJECTIVES

What It Is

Now, with your team in place, you and your team start to break down the project into objectives. In project management lingo, these might be called subobjectives, because they are subordinate to the project's overall objective (such as constructing a building or reducing accounts receivable). Kerzner (p. 380) says the characteristics of project objectives must be:

- Specific, not general
- Not overly complex
- Measurable, tangible, and verifiable
- Appropriate level; challenging
- Realistic and attainable
- Established within resource bounds
- Consistent with resources available or anticipated
- Consistent with organizational plans, policies, and procedures

The objectives go in the rectangle on the lower left-hand corner of the One-Page Project Manager, which is highlighted in Figure 5.5. In our filled-in One-Page Project Manager on page 69, the objectives are: building complete (completing the construction of the building), systems operational (meaning that all the systems within the building are operational and working the way they were specified to work), and people deployed (all the people who will be working in the distribution center are hired, and that they are trained

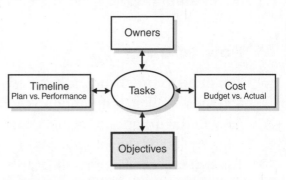

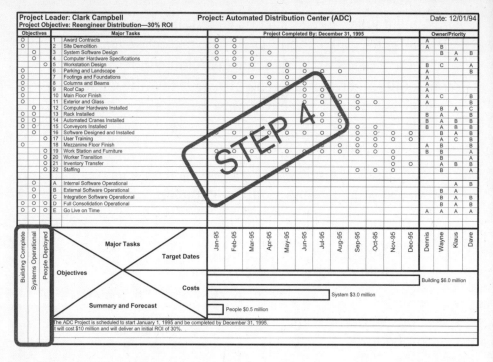

FIGURE 5.5   *The One-Page Project Manager—Step 4.*

Copyright O.C. Tanner 2007. **To customize this document, download it to your hard drive from the following web site: www.onepageprojectmanager.com.** The document can be opened, edited, and printed using Microsoft Excel or another popular spreadsheet application.

on the new equipment and ready to have the center up and running).

How to Do It

You need to break the project down into subobjectives, and these typically number no more than three or four. As with the number of owners, and the use of the One-Page Project Manager, we are on a quest for simplicity. The $10 million Automated Distribution Center we built at O.C. Tanner had only three subobjectives attached to the project.

52

You need to ask yourself and your team, what's really important with this project? Is being on time really vital? Is cutting costs? What do you really need to achieve with this project?

Every competent project manager knows he or she must balance these project variables, each dependent on the other. The three variables, or triple constraints of a project are:

1. *Time:* This refers to the time for the various steps involved with a project and ultimately the time it takes to complete the entire project.

2. *Resources:* These are the assets, the resources you have at your disposal to complete the project. Usually, the most important resources are people and money.

3. *Scope:* In *Project Management Memory Jogger,* by Paula Martin and Karen Tate, there is this definition of scope: "The project scope defines who the customers are, the final deliverables that will be produced for them, and the criteria that the customers will use to judge their satisfaction with the deliverables" (p. 53).

How do these three factors play a role in project management? They work together, and when one gets out of balance the whole can come tumbling down. To prevent that, you, the project manager, have to make adjustments in the other two factors.

For example, say you were building a house for you and your family. If you have a mortgage and can't add any more to the down payment, the money you are working with is fixed. In that case, if you want to, say, add a bathroom to the house, something else will have to give, perhaps the size of the master bedroom or the number of closets— whatever. You have to adjust one variable to accommodate a change in another. Balance and equilibrium must be maintained.

TIP When determining your objectives, find a few that are a litmus test for your project. What are the major accomplishments you want? When you can answer this question, determining the project's objectives will prove relatively easy.

One of the benefits of creating a One-Page Project Manager is that, as you work through it, you will gain an increasing understanding of the project, and you and your team will discover, through this process, those aspects of the project that will need the majority of your attention and which are less critical.

Some objectives are so obvious; They don't need to be enumerated on the One-Page Project Manager, such as being on time and on budget. The three objectives on the One-Page Project Manager that we just discussed (building complete, systems operational, people deployed) were all discussed by the team and agreed to. They're not profound, unexpected, or difficult to comprehend, which is why they are good objectives. They are simple, direct, to the point, easily understood, and, of course, valued. They really are, at their most basic, what this project is about.

STEP 5: MAJOR PROJECT TASKS

What It Is

In Figure 5.6, you'll see highlighted, on the left side of the One-Page Project Manager, a rectangle that encompasses the major project tasks. Of all the components of the One-Page Project Manager, this is arguably the most important. Think of the tasks as what it's going to take to finish the project. A $10 million project is really just the sum total of 50 $200,000 projects or 10 $1 million projects that are coordinated and combined to add up to the final project.

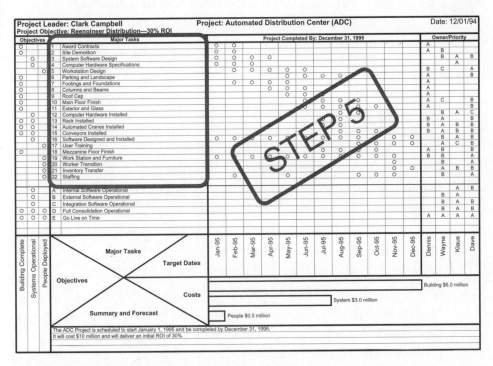

FIGURE 5.6   *The One-Page Project Manager—Step 5.*

Copyright O.C. Tanner 2007. **To customize this document, download it to your hard drive from the following web site: www.onepageprojectmanager.com.** The document can be opened, edited, and printed using Microsoft Excel or another popular spreadsheet application.

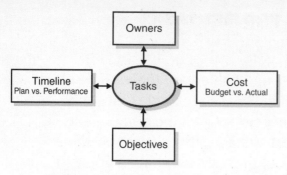

In the completed form on page 93, I list the 22 major tasks we, as a team, identified. These include: Award Contracts, Site Demolition, System Software Design, Computer Hardware Specifications, Workstation Design, Parking and Landscape, Footings and Foundation, Columns and Beams, Roof Cap, and others.

TIP To be effective, each task must be of a manageable size, where the project is of a size that one person can be the lead.

How to Do It

With the One-Page Project Manager, you take a large task, like that of constructing a building, and break that down into smaller ones—such as award contracts, site demolition, and so on. In the case of the distribution center, the smaller tasks each appear on the highest level One-Page Project Manager, the one we are focusing on in this book. Each of these—Award Contracts, Site Demolition, System Software Design, Computer Hardware Specifications—would, in turn, have its own One-Page Project Manager, or be supported by other project management software.

For large projects, you need to align your tasks with those shown in the project management software programs necessary for various parts of your project. The building aspects of our project were carefully detailed using the program Primavera P3. The software and hardware components were thoroughly constructed in Microsoft Project. The One-Page Project Manager does not replace these often necessary and valuable tools. It "sits on top" as the highest level learning, coordinating, and then communicating document. Often, with smaller projects, you and your team don't need such help and can identify the tasks yourselves.

KEY CONCEPT You absolutely need buy-in from all participants. This is especially true for the tasks you delineate in the One-Page Project Manager. Each task will be assigned at least one owner, and if owners and their teams are not in agreement with what is specified on the One-Page Project Manager, the project is in jeopardy. Be sure to seek input and buy-in from owners, others inside the organizations, outside consultants, and anyone else with a stake in the project.

In this book, we're focusing on the top-most level, the One-Page Project Manager that would be looked at by senior management. Let's take the Reducing Accounts Receivable project that I mentioned earlier. A task might be: the analysis of studying the creditworthiness of customers. If your customers aren't credit worthy, chances are you will have trouble collecting your accounts receivable. We might have a One-Page Project Manager just for the task of analyzing the creditworthiness of customers. It would have its own task breakdown. This is what I mean by having multiple layers of One-Page Project Managers.

In addition to being of manageable size, each task should be distinct—separate from other tasks. You can't have accountability if it is hard to tell where one task ends and another begins.

Constructing a building gets the top-most One-Page Project Manager, and constructing the footings and foundations would be a task listed on this One-Page Project Manager, and could get its own One-Page Project Manager. On the footings and foundations level, there might be a task involving building the wood forms needed to pour the concrete into. Constructing the foundation would be a distinct task on the top-most One-Page Project Manager, and constructing the forms would be a distinct task on the One-Page Project Manager that is just for the building's foundation.

 Tasks should be measurable in terms of their progress so you can gauge their advancement and report on them in the One-Page Project Manager.

Also, you need to have enough such tasks, but not too many. Too many makes it hard to track what's going on and to get the big picture, while too few makes each task harder to manage. How many tasks are not too many but enough?

Rule of thumb: Try to average two to three tasks per reporting period for the length of the project. If the project will run nine months, 18 or so tasks are probably right. A two-year project would have approximately 48 tasks. On the other end of the spectrum, don't divide the project into too few tasks. Try to make the tasks last no longer than half the project's total time horizon. If the project will last four months, then there should be a minimum of two tasks, and probably more. Most projects, in fact, should probably be divided into at least monthly increments.

As I've noted before, communication is the key to project management, and defining the major project tasks. Creating these definitions should be a team effort; one person—you or anyone else, should not dictate them. As the project is discussed, you and your team will probably get a sense of what the reasonable task divisions are. As with the name of the project, it's probably best to hold off for a while defining the tasks, until you and your team get a better understanding of what's involved.

One of the reasons this step is so critical is that it involves not just the tasks, but also the owners. As you create tasks, you have to align them with the project's owners. If one owner is particularly strong in one area, say financial controls, and the others are particularly weak in this area, then the financial wizard will likely take on many or most tasks involving finances. But if there are a number of tasks involving finances, he or she may not be able to take them all on. In this case, some tasks with relatively minor financial control aspects to them might be given to some of the other owners, while the bulk of the financially oriented tasks goes to the team member who knows about finances. What you've done here is align the tasks with owners. This is critical for the project's success.

CONTINUOUS IMPROVEMENT

Before we go further, let me take a detour to discuss a couple of important points.

When building the One-Page Project Manager, it's always fair to revisit earlier steps. Like most things in life, this tool is not carved in stone. If, as the project progresses, you find the need to change something or tweak something else, do so. Be open to continuous improvement. The One-Page Project Manager is a tool designed to help you communicate aspects of a project to those with interests in the project. It is not something that should dictate how a project progresses or is managed. Bend the tool to fit the project, not the project to fit the tool.

The One-Page Project Manager offers you just that—one page to write all the information you need to convey. That's not much space, which I consider one of its advantages. It will force you to be descriptive, efficient, and precise with your language. Instead of, "build the mezzanine floor and finish it," you might have, "Mezzanine Floor Finish." Keep it succinct: "Rack Installed," "Roof Cap."

Avoid jargon, acronyms, and abbreviations. Keep in mind that this One-Page Project Manager will have to communicate up, down, and out, and not all of those audiences know the entire lingo you and your colleagues know. If you want to use this tool to its maximum effectiveness as a means to communicate, use language and a vocabulary everyone can understand.

Accept the fact that you don't have much space to be explanatory. View that as a blessing, as something that will help you communicate better. The very act of having to be so brief in your descriptions usually makes you more exacting. Your communications should improve with the One-Page Project Manager.

One more thing: The One-Page Project Manager is just that—one page. It cannot show all aspects of a project and is not designed to do so. That means important aspects of project management are not represented by this tool, perhaps most notably, dependencies and capacity planning. If task 7 is dependent on the completion of task 4, you won't know this from the One-Page Project Manager. The owners, when they make their presentations to upper management, will mention this because it will not be found in the One-Page Project Manager. The capacity of the system to deal with scarcity of resources—for example, there are an insufficient number of people available to do a task—will also not be represented in the tool. Owners must take responsibility for getting all the resources they need.

What's important here is acknowledging the limitations of the tool. It cannot depict everything about a project. It doesn't cover all aspects of a project. It is but one page. Yet, that page conveys virtually all the pertinent information that senior management needs to know about a project (up communication), much of the information of interest to peers (out communication), and those at lower levels (down communication).

STEP 6: ALIGNING TASKS WITH OBJECTIVES

What It Is

In this step, you check to make sure the tasks on your list will, when completed, produce the objectives you are aiming for. Note in Figure 5.7, Objectives and Major Project Tasks are highlighted in blue. This is symbolic of the interrelatedness of objectives with tasks.

How to Do It

Here is where you may need to be flexible, as we just discussed. As you go through your tasks and objectives, it's essential that the two match up (Figure 5.8). You may well find that this process of analysis reveals certain

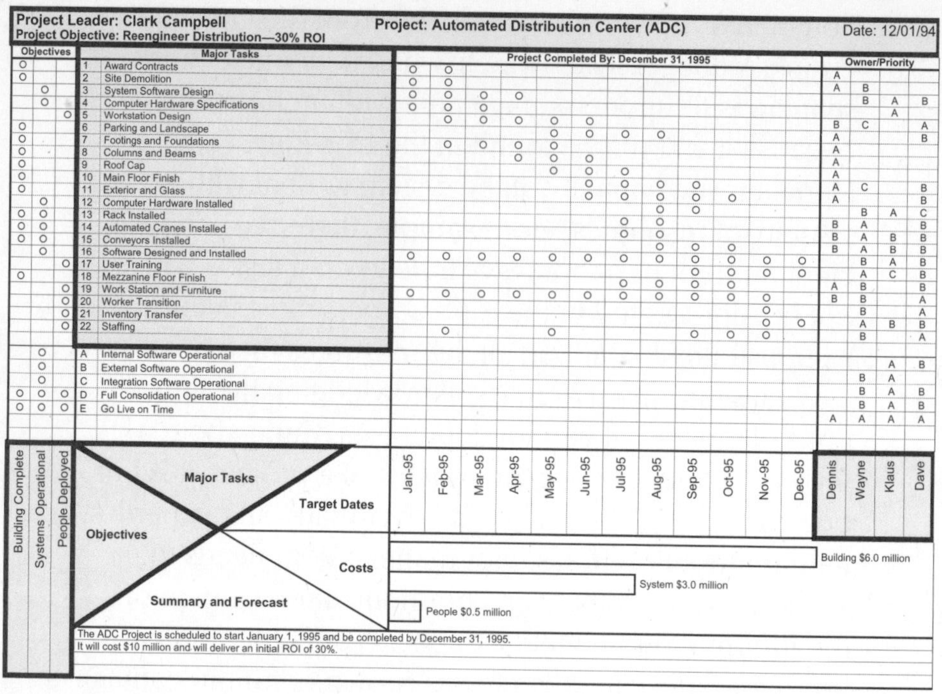

Project Leader: Clark Campbell				Project: Automated Distribution Center (ADC)		Date: 12/01/94

Project Objective: Reengineer Distribution—30% ROI

The following is a reproduction of the One-Page Project Manager form showing Objectives, Major Tasks, Project Completed By: December 31, 1995, and Owner/Priority columns.

Objectives					#	Major Tasks	Jan-95	Feb-95	Mar-95	Apr-95	May-95	Jun-95	Jul-95	Aug-95	Sep-95	Oct-95	Nov-95	Dec-95	Dennis	Wayne	Klaus	Dave
O					1	Award Contracts	O	O											A			
O					2	Site Demolition	O	O											A	B		
		O			3	System Software Design	O	O	O	O									A	B		
	O				4	Computer Hardware Specifications	O	O	O										B	A	B	
			O		5	Workstation Design	O	O	O											A		
O					6	Parking and Landscape				O	O	O							B	C		A
O					7	Footings and Foundations			O	O	O	O							A			B
O					8	Columns and Beams				O	O	O							A			
O					9	Roof Cap					O	O							A			
O					10	Main Floor Finish					O	O	O						A			
O					11	Exterior and Glass						O	O	O	O				A	C		B
	O				12	Computer Hardware Installed								O	O	O			A			B
O	O				13	Rack Installed								O	O				B	A	B	C
O	O				14	Automated Cranes Installed							O	O					B	A	B	B
O	O				15	Conveyors Installed								O	O				B	A	B	B
		O			16	Software Designed and Installed	O	O	O	O	O	O	O	O	O	O			B	A	B	B
			O		17	User Training									O	O	O	O	B	A	B	B
O					18	Mezzanine Floor Finish								O	O	O	O	O	A	C		B
			O		19	Work Station and Furniture	O	O	O	O	O	O	O	O	O	O			A	B		A
			O		20	Worker Transition										O			B	B		A
			O		21	Inventory Transfer										O	O	O		B		A
			O		22	Staffing		O			O				O	O	O		A	B	B	A
	O				A	Internal Software Operational																
	O				B	External Software Operational															A	B
	O				C	Integration Software Operational													B	A		
O	O	O			D	Full Consolidation Operational													B	A		B
O	O	O	O		E	Go Live on Time													B	A	A	A
																		A	A	A	A

Major Tasks — Target Dates — Objectives — Costs — Summary and Forecast

Building Complete / Systems Operational / People Deployed

Costs:
- Building $6.0 million
- System $3.0 million
- People $0.5 million

The ADC Project is scheduled to start January 1, 1995 and be completed by December 31, 1995.
It will cost $10 million and will deliver an initial ROI of 30%.

FIGURE 5.7   *The One-Page Project Manager—tasks and objectives are interrelated.*

anomalies, inconsistencies, or things missing. Let's say you are considering the objective, "Building Complete." You've gone through your tasks and listed them. But when you go through this step, aligning the tasks with objectives, you may find you don't have any tasks that relate to completing the building. Go back and add some.

This process of alignment is not something done once and left forever. As you work your way through the project, with each step, it is natural that you reevaluate succeeding steps. Think of the One-Page Project Manager as a connective web that supports the entire project. With each step,

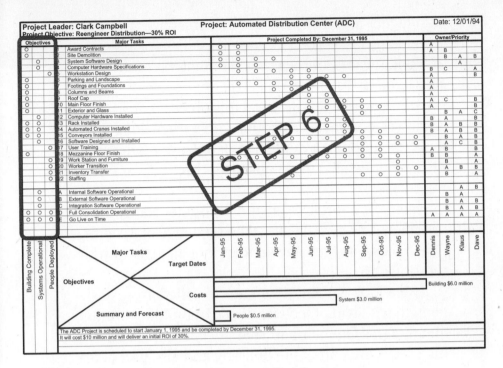

FIGURE 5.8 *The One-Page Project Manager—Step 6.*

you have the opportunity to improve. This is the same idea as continuous improvement in manufacturing.

In fact, I firmly believe that one of the greatest strengths of the One-Page Project Manager is that it has continuous improvement embedded in its construction. Don't fight this; instead, use it to your advantage.

Having said this, let me make clear that over analysis is the death of many projects. As I noted before, we at O.C. Tanner went to school to study project management, hired consultants, and bought books. At one time, we had 25 forms. Our project management program died under its own weight.

In Figure 5.8 where you see the Objectives aligned with Major Tasks, you can see the process of alignment at work. Award Contracts is a task that has to do with the Building Complete objective, and you can see there is a circle where this task and this objective intersect. Awarding contracts has nothing do with making the systems operational or deploying people, so there are no circles connecting these objectives to the Award Contracts task.

System Software Design and Computer Hardware specifications directly affect the objective of Systems Operational, so they have circles that align them with this objective.

Take a look at the task of Rack Installed. Note it is aligned with two objectives, those of Building Complete and Systems Operational. That's because these 30-foot-high racks are part of the building and also part of the systems we were developing. User Training, not surprisingly, is aligned with the People Deployed objective, because the people who are being deployed in the building have to first be trained.

Some of the tasks are aligned with two objectives, but most are aligned with just one; *all tasks are aligned with at least one objective.* If a task cannot be aligned to an objective, there's no point in doing the task and it should not be included in the One-Page Project Manager.

Let me give another quick example of how we aligned particular tasks with an objective. This was with our accounts receivable reduction project. The objective in question was to reduce accounts receivable. While setting the project up, we realized that in the past, all our energy toward reaching this objective was focused on collections. We tried to get the collections department to be more efficient and effective, thinking it was the heart of the problem.

But as we studied the accounts receivable process, we came to a new realization: The process was more complex and involved more folks than just the collections department. The One-Page Project Manager forced us to analyze the entire quote-to-cash process, and we ended up dividing it into four subprocesses:

1. *Selling* (selling the product or service)
2. Which leads to the *Setup* (recording the sale, setting up the account, doing credit checks, etc.)
3. Which leads to *Invoicing* (creating and sending the invoice)
4. Which finally leads to *Collecting*

What we had been ignoring were the first three steps of the process (selling, setup, and invoicing) and putting all our energy into the last step (collecting). But, in fact, all the sets contributed to the problem of us having a large number of accounts receivable at any given time.

Products and services were sold to customers who had unique and diverse payables requirements. The salespeople were paid commissions when awards were shipped and invoiced, not when sales were paid for, so the motivation of the salespeople was quickly diluted following shipment. The program setup process didn't always do a good job at meeting the invoice formatting demands of customers. Customers would want certain formats or information that our invoices did not always provide, and when the formatting wasn't right, they delayed payment. And the invoicing process often made mistakes by sending invoices to the wrong person or department, or having wrong pricing or other information. No wonder the collections department was having such a hard time collecting!

To use the imagery of Stephen R. Covey, author of *The Seven Habits of Highly Effective People,* we were hacking at branches rather than focusing on roots.

To reduce our accounts receivable, we had to improve *all* our processes. It is this type of insight that can come during the creation of a One-Page Project Manager.

STEP 7: TARGET DATES

What It Is

With this step, shown in Figure 5.9 as a rectangle running left to right near the bottom of the One-Page Project Manager, we break down the timeline into discrete steps. This section is broken into monthly increments during the year 1995. You don't have to break a project down into monthly increments—I've done them every two weeks, once a month, once every two months, and once every three months—but monthly is, from my experience, the most common.

How to Do It

The first step here is to evaluate the total time horizon for the project. Then, we break down the timeline into measurable time buckets—what we referred to earlier when we discussed how to break down a project's time variable.

Before you commit to the timeline, think carefully about what you are committing to. When you let everyone know the project's timeline and time incre-

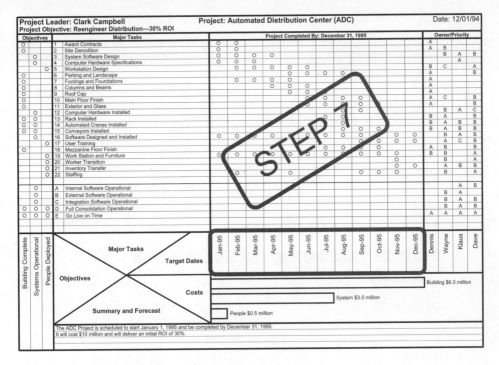

FIGURE 5.9   *The One-Page Project Manager—Step 7.*

ments, you become responsible for meeting them. As with tasks, you need buy-in from all concerned. You cannot impose a timeline or deadline and expect everyone to jump up and down and say thank you. A timeline is an imposition and obligation and that's why you need to discuss it with all who will be responsible for meeting the timeline. You need to have their agreement that the timeline is doable and that they will perform and meet it.

A technique to use is to take the final completion date, which is written at the top of the One-Page Project Manager, and work backward from that date,

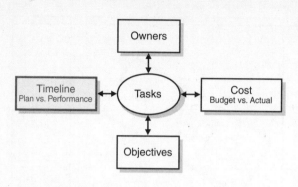

going through all the steps in the project. See if when you get to the beginning that there is enough time to do everything. If not, you know the timeline has to be adjusted.

STEP 8: ALIGNING TASKS TO THE TIMELINE

What It Is

What we are now doing is aligning or connecting the timeline with the tasks. The blue highlights in Figure 5.10 show previously completed steps. Particular attention is now given to the cross-over between Major Tasks and Target Dates.

How to Do It

We decide how long each task will take. Then we place an empty circle in the boxes alongside the task. If the task will take seven months and the time buckets are in monthly increments, then there will be seven circles next to this task. As each task is completed, the aligned circle is filled in.

Let's look at Figure 5.11 where we have these circles in place. The first task, Award Contracts, has two dots, in January and February. This means there are two months to complete this task and it should be finished by the end of February. Two lines below is the task relating to

Project Leader: Clark Campbell
Project Objective: Reengineer Distribution—30% ROI
Project: Automated Distribution Center (ADC)
Date: 12/01/94

Project Completed By: December 31, 1995

#	Major Tasks
1	Award Contracts
2	Site Demolition
3	System Software Design
4	Computer Hardware Specifications
5	Workstation Design
6	Parking and Landscape
7	Footings and Foundations
8	Columns and Beams
9	Roof Cap
10	Main Floor Finish
11	Exterior and Glass
12	Computer Hardware Installed
13	Rack Installed
14	Automated Cranes Installed
15	Conveyors Installed
16	Software Designed and Installed
17	User Training
18	Mezzanine Floor Finish
19	Work Station and Furniture
20	Worker Transition
21	Inventory Transfer
22	Staffing
A	Internal Software Operational
B	External Software Operational
C	Integration Software Operational
D	Full Consolidation Operational
E	Go Live on Time

Objectives: Building Complete, Systems Operational, People Deployed

Major Tasks / Target Dates / Objectives / Costs / Summary and Forecast

Months: Jan-95, Feb-95, Mar-95, Apr-95, May-95, Jun-95, Jul-95, Aug-95, Sep-95, Oct-95, Nov-95, Dec-95

Owner/Priority: Dennis, Wayne, Klaus, Dave

Building $6.0 million
System $3.0 million
People $0.5 million

The ADC Project is scheduled to start January 1, 1995 and be completed by December 31, 1995.
It will cost $10 million and will deliver an initial ROI of 30%.

FIGURE 5.10   *The One-Page Project Manager—timeline breakdown.*

Copyright O.C. Tanner 2007. **To customize this document, download it to your hard drive from the following web site: www.onepageprojectmanager.com.** The document can be opened, edited, and printed using Microsoft Excel or another popular spreadsheet application.

System Software Design. This too starts at the beginning of the project, January, but has four dots. It is being given four months to be completed.

Consider the task on line 6, Parking and Landscape. That also has been given four months to be completed, but the first circle is placed in the May column. This means we don't expect this task to start until May, which makes sense since we would expect to complete other tasks first, such as the Footings and Foundations and the System Software Design.

Look at the last task listed, Staffing on line 22. Note how haphazard this is in terms of the circles aligned

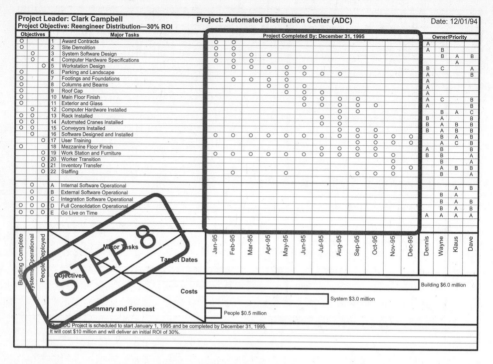

FIGURE 5.11   *The One-Page Project Manager—Step 8.*

with it. There's a circle in February, and the next one is May, and then there are three starting in September, but none in December. That's because Staffing isn't done on a regular basis but on an irregular basis, as needed. User Training, another task, doesn't get started until late in the project, namely September. That's logical because there's no need to start training people to work the building's equipment and systems until the completion of the building is near.

STEP 9: ALIGNING TASKS TO OWNERS

What It Is

Note that on Figure 5.12, the highlighted areas call out previously completed steps. Attention is drawn to the top right section of the form. With this step, we align tasks to their owners and assign priorities among owners when a task has more than one owner.

How to Do It

Tasks have owners. It is possible for a task to have more than one owner. Rarely will a task have more than three

Project Leader: Clark Campbell	Project: Automated Distribution Center (ADC)	Date: 12/01/94
Project Objective: Reengineer Distribution—30% ROI		

Objectives	#	Major Tasks	Project Completed By: December 31, 1995	Owner/Priority (Dennis, Wayne, Klaus, Dave)
	1	Award Contracts	○ ○	A
	2	Site Demolition	○ ○	A B
	3	System Software Design	○ ○ ○ ○	B A B
	4	Computer Hardware Specifications	○ ○ ○	A
	5	Workstation Design	○ ○ ○ ○	B C A
	6	Parking and Landscape	○ ○ ○ ○	A B
	7	Footings and Foundations	○ ○ ○ ○	A
	8	Columns and Beams	○ ○ ○	A
	9	Roof Cap	○ ○ ○	A
	10	Main Floor Finish	○ ○ ○ ○	A C B
	11	Exterior and Glass	○ ○ ○ ○ ○	A B
	12	Computer Hardware Installed	○ ○	B A C
	13	Rack Installed	○ ○	B A B
	14	Automated Cranes Installed	○ ○	B A B B
	15	Conveyors Installed	○ ○ ○	B A B B
	16	Software Designed and Installed	○ ○ ○ ○ ○ ○ ○ ○ ○ ○	B A B
	17	User Training	○ ○ ○ ○ ○	A C B
	18	Mezzanine Floor Finish	○ ○ ○ ○	A B B
	19	Work Station and Furniture	○ ○ ○ ○ ○ ○ ○ ○ ○	B B A
	20	Worker Transition	○	B A
	21	Inventory Transfer	○ ○	A B B
	22	Staffing	○ ○ ○ ○ ○	B A
	A	Internal Software Operational		A B
	B	External Software Operational		B A
	C	Integration Software Operational		B A B
	D	Full Consolidation Operational		B A B
	E	Go Live on Time		A A A A

Building Complete | Systems Operational | People Deployed

Major Tasks / Target Dates

Objectives / Costs

Summary and Forecast

Jan-95 | Feb-95 | Mar-95 | Apr-95 | May-95 | Jun-95 | Jul-95 | Aug-95 | Sep-95 | Oct-95 | Nov-95 | Dec-95 | Dennis | Wayne | Klaus | Dave

Building $6.0 million
System $3.0 million
People $0.5 million

The ADC Project is scheduled to start January 1, 1995 and be completed by December 31, 1995.
It will cost $10 million and will deliver an initial ROI of 30%.

FIGURE 5.12 *The One-Page Project Manager—how Step 9 works.*

owners. But, no matter how many owners per task, a priority between owners must be set. There is almost always *one* main owner. The letter A on the One-Page Project Manager designates that owner. If there is a sub-owner, that person is designated by a B, while a third owner gets a C. But, let me emphasize again, you should almost *never have more than one principle owner for each task*. Each task must have someone on the team who has taken ultimate responsibility.

If an owner has primary responsibility for such-and-such task, where the row and column for that task and owner intersect, there will be an A. If another owner has secondary responsibility, he or she will get a B where their column and the task's row intersect. And for a third owner, a C is placed in the same way. You can see these in Figure 5.13 where the Owner/Priority section is filled in.

Some tasks have only one owner, so the row for that task will only have one letter in the Owner/Priority section and that letter will, of course, be an A.

KEY CONCEPT Some projects are small enough that each task has only one owner. In this case, where there are no priorities being set, circles instead of letters are used designating which owner owns which task.

In our filled-in example at the end of the chapter, you'll see that the first task (line 1), Award Contracts, has one owner, Dennis. With one owner, he gets an A in the box for that task. The third task (line 3), System Software Design, has three owners: Klaus is the A owner and Wayne and Dave are B owners. This means that Klaus is ultimately in charge, but Wayne and Dave also have responsibility for the success of the task. Since

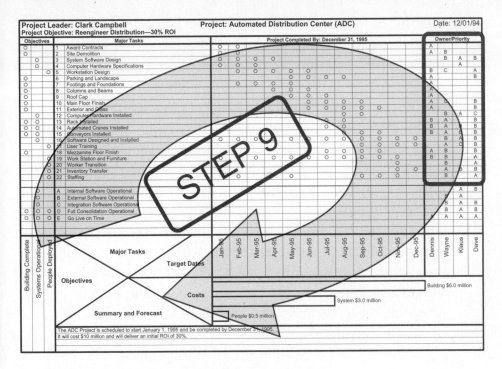

FIGURE 5.13 *The One-Page Project Manager—Step 9.*

both are B owners, they are equally responsible. You can have more than one B or C owners, but *you should strongly avoid having more than one A owner.* Main Floor Finish task (line 10) has three owners: Dennis has top priority as indicated by his A; Dave, with his B, has secondary responsibility; and Wayne has tertiary responsibility, which is why he gets a C. Klaus is not involved and therefore gets no letter connected to this task.

Who owns what is decided through a process of negotiation between members of the team, with you providing leadership and, if need be, mediation. At the end of this step, everyone knows what they own and where they stand, in the pecking order, for each task.

The process of divvying up ownership is an exercise in team building, and effective project managers use the One-Page Project Manager in this way. If you have a team where members try to avoid ownership of the various tasks, you have a weak team that needs to be trained in teamwork or replaced. Ideally, when going through the project's tasks and looking for owners, you will have team members weighing in, holding up their hands, and volunteering to take on responsibility. When they see that one member perhaps has more A ownership tasks than others, the others might volunteer to be B owners on those tasks and pledge to help out. This is, of course, the ideal.

The reality might be different. You might have a team whose members do little to help one another and who are looking to do as little as possible. This exercise is a good diagnostic for understanding the strengths of your team and whether you need to use your team building skills to strengthen the team.

As the project leader, you need to keep your owners focused on successfully completing their tasks. You can't suffer whiners, who complain about how much work they have or the lack of cooperation they are receiving from others or whatever other excuse they might devise. Nor can you suffer victims, who blame others or make excuses focusing around the notion that when things go bad, it's not their fault. Once an owner is decided and has signed off on a task, he or she owns it. Period. No matter what. No excuses, no complaints, no whining.

Also, as the project leader, you need to encourage communication between all levels. Yes, I keep coming back to communication, but that's because it is the most essential ingredient for the success of any project. It's okay for a subordinate to go over your head and talk to your superior, if that team member feels the need to communicate directly with the superior. What you want is open dialog. You want your people to feel free to communicate—both good and bad news. The One-Page Project Manager helps foster an environment where communication is encouraged between all involved parties. It opens the door and invites people into your project. A successful project is not managed in a closed office, but only in an open one.

KEY CONCEPT A key to the success of any project is transparency of communication. Communication must be open, devoid of agendas, and viewable by all constituents.

STEP 10: SUBJECTIVE TASKS

What It Is

This is the portion of the One-Page Project Manager that deals with subjective or qualitative tasks. There are parts of every project that do not easily lend themselves to quantitative analysis on a timeline. You'll find this section open across the entire middle of the page (Figure 5.14).

Software performance is often in this category. We had an ERP project we called Cornerstone. Part of that project involved billing screens that would come up on workers' computers. It wasn't easy to say whether the time it took for the billing screen to come up was adequate or not adequate. This was a judgment call. We

Project Leader: Clark Campbell **Project: Automated Distribution Center (ADC)** Date: 12/01/94

Project Objective: Reengineer Distribution—30% ROI

Major Tasks (Project Completed By: December 31, 1995):

#	Major Tasks
1	Award Contracts
2	Site Demolition
3	System Software Design
4	Computer Hardware Specifications
5	Workstation Design
6	Parking and Landscape
7	Footings and Foundations
8	Columns and Beams
9	Roof Cap
10	Main Floor Finish
11	Exterior and Glass
12	Computer Hardware Installed
13	Rack Installed
14	Automated Cranes Installed
15	Conveyors Installed
16	Software Designed and Installed
17	User Training
18	Mezzanine Floor Finish
19	Work Station and Furniture
20	Worker Transition
21	Inventory Transfer
22	Staffing
A	Internal Software Operational
B	External Software Operational
C	Integration Software Operational
D	Full Consolidation Operational
E	Go Live on Time

Objectives: Building Complete · Systems Operational · People Deployed

Major Tasks / Target Dates / Objectives / Costs / Summary and Forecast

Target Dates (months): Jan-95, Feb-95, Mar-95, Apr-95, May-95, Jun-95, Jul-95, Aug-95, Sep-95, Oct-95, Nov-95, Dec-95

Owner/Priority: Dennis, Wayne, Klaus, Dave

Costs:
- Building $6.0 million
- System $3.0 million
- People $0.5 million

The ADC Project is scheduled to start January 1, 1995 and be completed by December 31, 1995. It will cost $10 million and will deliver an initial ROI of 30%.

FIGURE 5.14 *The One-Page Project Manager—tasks have owners.*

could have said that if the screen took more than two seconds to come up, the performance was inadequate, but the truth was, we preferred the screen to come up within 0.5 seconds, though one or even two seconds was acceptable, at least if it didn't always take that long.

What about cell phone reception? It might be unacceptable to have a cell phone call be disconnected, but what about when a call has static or otherwise has a connection where it is hard to hear the other caller? When is cell phone reception acceptable and when is it unacceptable? Situations like this are subjective and hard to objectively quantify.

Not everything in life—or in projects—is black or white. This section of the project manager recognizes this and uses three colors to depict it. Inadequate performance is given a red—boxes next to the task are filled with bright red ink. In such situations, the unacceptable performance may affect the project's total performance. Where performance for these subjective tasks is clearly adequate, a strong green is used to fill in the boxes. Here, the performance will not adversely affect the total project. And for those times when one isn't quite sure whether things are going well enough, yellow is used. This is when performance or results are questionable and the total project's performance may or may not be affected.

How to Do It

In Figure 5.15, where the Subjective Tasks are filled in, you will find five tasks listed: Internal Software Operational, External Software Operational, Integration Software Operational, Full Consolidation Operational, and Go Live on Time. The first three of these all are related to software and, as we just discussed, it's often hard to quantify how well software performs. Yet, of course, software can be vital (which it certainly was with our Automated Distribution Center); you can't ignore it. It is listed in the One-Page Project Manager because it cannot be ignored, but it is among the subjective major tasks because it is so hard to quantify. Full Consolidation Operational is another example. This line shows how well the combined connected system is operating. We see the progress of the Internal and External Software, the connecting or Integration Software, and now the full system as a whole. The last subjective task, Go Live on Time,

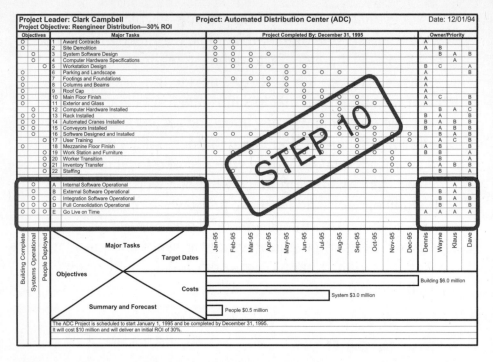

FIGURE 5.15   *The One-Page Project Manager—Step 10.*

refers to the project team's best judgment about getting the entire building and its systems operating and doing so according to the project's timeline.

Be aware that objectives and owners are aligned with these subjective tasks just as they are with tasks that are more quantifiable. These tasks must be tied to the project's main objectives and each must have at least one owner. You'll note that we broke our own rule of only one A owner per task. The One-Page Project Manager is *for projects*—not the other way around. It should accommodate your project—your project shouldn't accommodate the One-Page Project Manager.

STEP 11: COSTS

What It Is

In Figure 5.16, the rectangle in the lower right-hand side of the One-Page Project Manager is highlighted. This is where the budget is represented. The budget is dealt with in a simple, straightforward manner via bar graphs.

We've divided the budget into three parts: Building ($6.0 million), Systems ($3.0 million), and People ($0.5 million). These are simple bar graphs, and the length of each bar represents the amount of money for that part of the budget. Although the target dates are listed just above the budget

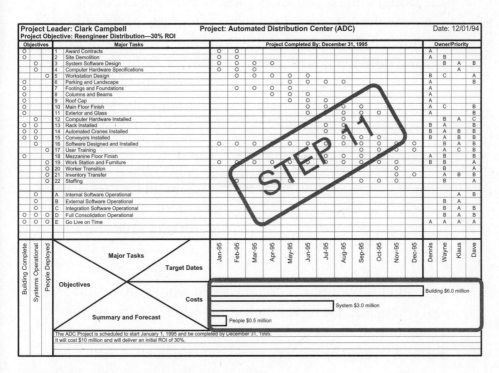

FIGURE 5.16   *The One-Page Project Manager—Step 11.*

lines, there is no relation between them. In fact, the budget stands alone; it is not related to the timeline, the objectives or the owners. The purpose of this budget graph is to give management a quick, easy-to-understand picture of where the budget is at any given time.

How to Do It

This is very simple. Just create bar graphs for each portion of the budget. Use green to show when the project is on budget, yellow when it is running over budget but recoverable, and red to show it is incurably over budget. It is vital that as you draw up the budget lines, you work closely with the accounting department so you are using accurate information.

Showing the budget on the One-Page Project Manager is easy; deriving it is much more difficult. Before you

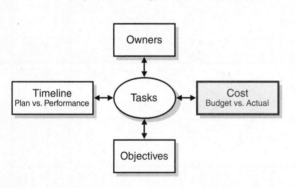

draw up the budget, be sure you know all your costs. For example, when drawing up the budget for the Automated Distribution Center, before we established the budget, we had agreements with our suppliers about what they would do, when, and for how much. Only when we knew our costs for certain were we willing to commit to a budget. Be sure you include all costs—software license, software support contracts, consultants, travel, training, and the like. Include provisions for incremental increases, such as those due to inflation or changes in the project.

Depending on how your organization operates, you may include in the budget "soft costs," such as internal people from your company who spend some or all of their time on your project.

You will also see that the three budget bars add to $9.5 million. We secured $10.0 million, which included $500,000 for unplanned contingencies.

STEP 12: SUMMARY AND FORECAST
What It Is

You have now completed all of your One-Page Project Manager except for the small Summary and Forecast section along the bottom of the page (Figure 5.17). With the first edition of your One-Page Project Manager, at the start of the project, this section is where you add the finishing touches to your plan. A good Summary at this point clears up any ambiguities or glaring questions and heads off potential future misunderstandings. Everybody should now be "reading from the same page"—both literally and metaphorically. It is here where you are committing yourself, saying this is your final plan.

Further, it is this completed edition of the One-Page Project Manager that is used to get final approval for your plan from upper management. It is the means by which you let management know the project's objectives, tasks, owners, budget, and timeline. It is easy to see that after management approves your project with the completed One-Page Project Manager, there is an easily communicated yet comprehensive meeting of the minds.

In subsequent One-Page Project Managers, you use the Summary to write down information about how the project is doing. It communicates how the project is doing at any given time and what you forecast for the

Project Leader: Clark Campbell   **Project: Automated Distribution Center (ADC)**   Date: 12/01/94

Project Objective: Reengineer Distribution—30% ROI

Objectives	#	Major Tasks	Project Completed By: December 31, 1995	Owner/Priority
	1	Award Contracts		A
	2	Site Demolition		A B
	3	System Software Design		B A B
	4	Computer Hardware Specifications		A
	5	Workstation Design		R C A
	6	Parking and Landscape		A B
	7	Footings and Foundations		A
	8	Columns and Beams		A
	9	Roof Cap		A
	10	Main Floor Finish		A C B
	11	Exterior and Glass		A B
	12	Computer Hardware Installed		B A C
	13	Rack Installed		B A B B
	14	Automated Cranes Installed		B A B B
	15	Conveyors Installed		B A B B
	16	Software Designed and Installed		B A B B
	17	User Training		A C B
	18	Mezzanine Floor Finish		A B B
	19	Work Station and Furniture		B B A
	20	Worker Transition		B A
	21	Inventory Transfer		A B B
	22	Staffing		B A
	A	Internal Software Operational		A B
	B	External Software Operational		B A B
	C	Integration Software Operational		B A B
	D	Full Consolidation Operational		B A B
	E	Go Live on Time		A A A A

Objectives (diagonal legend): Building Complete · Systems Operational · People Deployed

Major Tasks · Target Dates · Objectives · Costs · Summary and Forecast

Months: Jan-95, Feb-95, Mar-95, Apr-95, May-95, Jun-95, Jul-95, Aug-95, Sep-95, Oct-95, Nov-95, Dec-95

Owners: Dennis, Wayne, Klaus, Dave

Costs: Building $6.0 million · System $3.0 million · People $0.5 million

The ADC Project is scheduled to start January 1, 1995 and be completed by December 31, 1995. It will cost $10 million and will deliver an initial ROI of 30%.

FIGURE 5.17   *The One-Page Project Manager—how Step 12 works.*

Copyright O.C. Tanner 2007. **To customize this document, download it to your hard drive from the following web site: www.onepageprojectmanager.com.** The document can be opened, edited, and printed using Microsoft Excel or another popular spreadsheet application.

immediate future. Here, you write in complete sentences—not circles or sound bites—and be as succinct and comprehensive as possible.

How to Do It

The amount of space available for the summary is limited. On purpose. By limiting the space, it forces you to be selective about what you are describing and efficient in your discussion. Upper-level management isn't going to read lengthy treatises about different aspects of the project. They want to know what's going on and to learn that as quickly as possible (Figure 5.18).

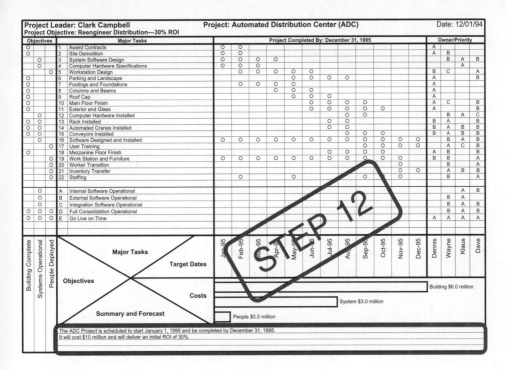

FIGURE 5.18   *The One-Page Project Manager—Step 12.*

Explain everything needed in the summary space. Do not attach additional pages or diagrams; management won't read them. This is a One-Page Project Manager and everything must be contained on this single piece of 8½-inch by 11-inch paper. This tool, when compiled correctly, can stand on its own.

The summary is important. It is where you communicate to your readers information that is not obvious or contained in the rest of the One-Page Project Manager. Here you answer the obvious, unanswered questions exposed by the completed information on the One-Page Project Manager. For example, if the project were over budget, that would be discussed here. If there are holdups because of problems with suppliers, so various aspects of the project are falling behind schedule, here's your chance to let your readers know why things are late.

This is your opportunity to make things clear, to set things straight, and to avoid misinterpretation. But don't tell management what is obvious. Don't say, "the System budget is running over budget," or "finishing the glass is running late." Such information, which is true, is also obvious to anyone reading the One-Page Project Manager.

 What the summary should be about is *why.* And *what you are going to do about it, what you expect to happen.*

The summary should focus on the whys that the One-Page Project Manager reveal: Why you are behind schedule, why you are over budget, why there are cost overruns, why this circle isn't filled in as it should be, and why that line is red instead of green.

After you explain the why, you explain what you are going to do about it and then you forecast what will happen.

The summary is where you explain to management those things that cannot be conveyed with any of the various integrated sections of the One-Page Project Manager.

THE TWELVE STEPS COME TOGETHER

Pages 85 through 107 provide a progressive full page view of each of the Twelve Steps as they are cumulatively completed. The first page outlines the area to be worked, and the following page shows the completed step. These pages continue until the full One-Page Project Manager is finished.

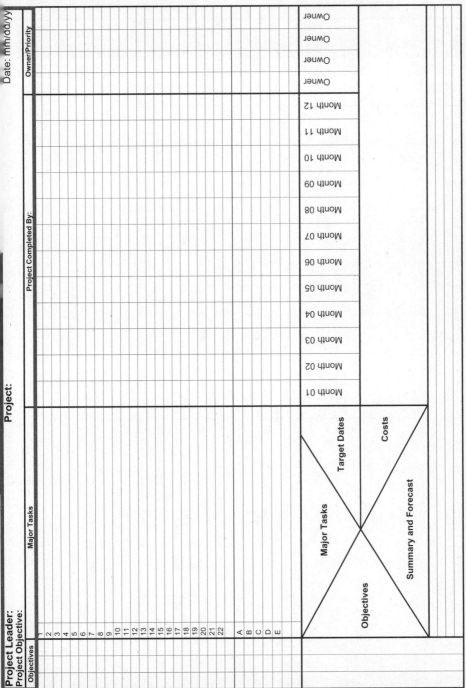

Project Leader:
Project Objective:

Project:

Date: mm/dd/yy

Objectives	Major Tasks	Project Completed By:											Owner/Priority

Month 01 | Month 02 | Month 03 | Month 04 | Month 05 | Month 06 | Month 07 | Month 08 | Month 09 | Month 10 | Month 11 | Month 12 | Owner | Owner | Owner | Owner

Objectives — 1, 2, 3, 4, 5, 6, 7, 8, 9, 10, 11, 12, 13, 14, 15, 16, 17, 18, 19, 20, 21, 22, A, B, C, D, E

Major Tasks / Objectives / Target Dates / Costs / Summary and Forecast

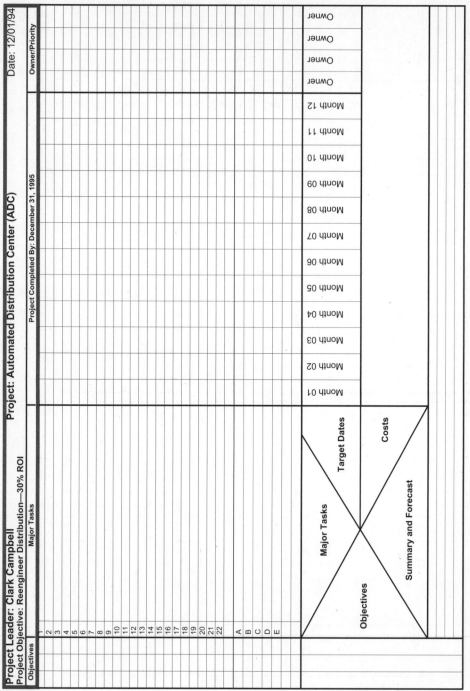

Project Leader: Clark Campbell

Project: Automated Distribution Center (ADC)

Date: 12/01/94

Project Objective: Reengineer Distribution—30% ROI

Project Completed By: December 31, 1995

Objectives	Major Tasks	Month 01	Month 02	Month 03	Month 04	Month 05	Month 06	Month 07	Month 08	Month 09	Month 10	Month 11	Month 12	Owner	Owner	Owner	Owner	Owner/Priority
	1																	
	2																	
	3																	
	4																	
	5																	
	6																	
	7																	
	8																	
	9																	
	10																	
	11																	
	12																	
	13																	
	14																	
	15																	
	16																	
	17																	
	18																	
	19																	
	20																	
	21																	
	22																	
	A																	
	B																	
	C																	
	D																	
	E																	

Major Tasks — Target Dates

Objectives — Costs

Summary and Forecast

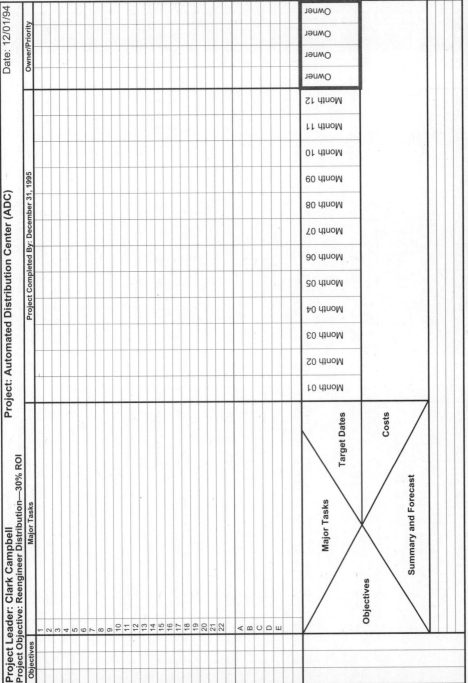

Project Leader: Clark Campbell
Project Objective: Reengineer Distribution—30% ROI
Project: Automated Distribution Center (ADC)
Date: 12/01/94
Project Completed By: December 31, 1995

Objectives

Major Tasks

1
2
3
4
5
6
7
8
9
10
11
12
13
14
15
16
17
18
19
20
21
22

A
B
C
D
E

Month 01
Month 02
Month 03
Month 04
Month 05
Month 06
Month 07
Month 08
Month 09
Month 10
Month 11
Month 12

Owner/Priority

Owner
Owner
Owner
Owner

Objectives
Major Tasks
Target Dates
Costs
Summary and Forecast

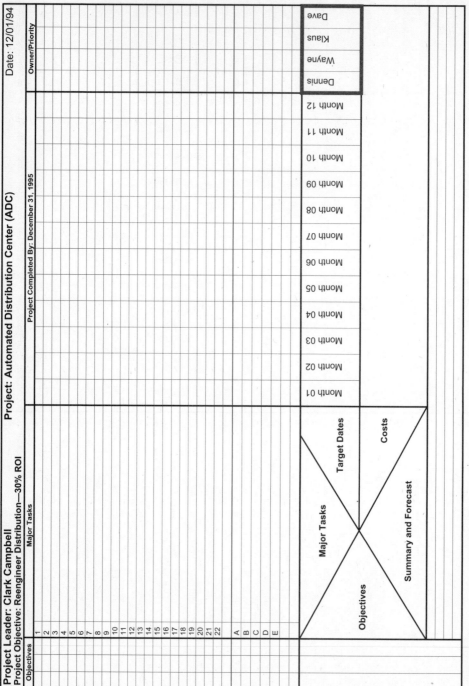

Project Leader: Clark Campbell

Project: Automated Distribution Center (ADC)

Date: 12/01/94

Project Objective: Reengineer Distribution—30% ROI

Project Completed By: December 31, 1995

Objectives	Major Tasks		Owner/Priority
1			
2			
3			
4			
5			
6			
7			
8			
9			
10			
11			
12			
13			
14			
15			
16			
17			
18			
19			
20			
21			
22			
A			
B			
C			
D			
E			

Month 01 | Month 02 | Month 03 | Month 04 | Month 05 | Month 06 | Month 07 | Month 08 | Month 09 | Month 10 | Month 11 | Month 12

Dennis | Wayne | Klaus | Dave

Objectives / Major Tasks / Target Dates / Costs / Summary and Forecast

88

Project Leader: Clark Campbell

Project: Automated Distribution Center (ADC)

Date: 12/01/94

Project Objective: Reengineer Distribution—30% ROI

Project Completed By: December 31, 1995

Objectives	Major Tasks	Month 01	Month 02	Month 03	Month 04	Month 05	Month 06	Month 07	Month 08	Month 09	Month 10	Month 11	Month 12	Dennis	Wayne	Klaus	Dave	Owner/Priority
	1																	
	2																	
	3																	
	4																	
	5																	
	6																	
	7																	
	8																	
	9																	
	10																	
	11																	
	12																	
	13																	
	14																	
	15																	
	16																	
	17																	
	18																	
	19																	
	20																	
	21																	
	22																	
A																		
B																		
C																		
D																		
E																		

Major Tasks

Target Dates

Objectives

Costs

Summary and Forecast

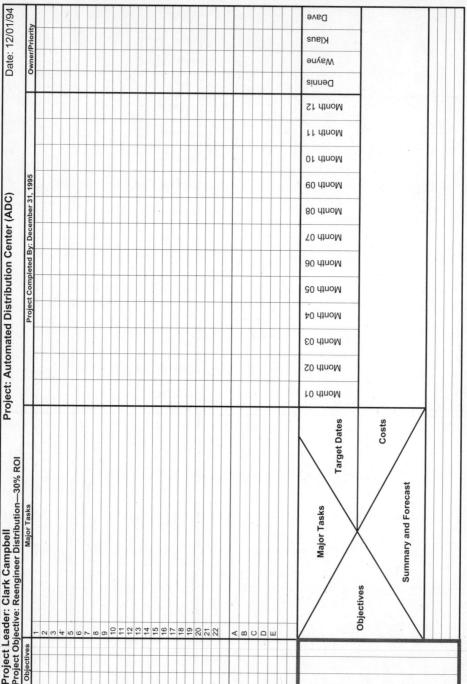

Project Leader: Clark Campbell   **Project: Automated Distribution Center (ADC)**   Date: 12/01/94

Project Objective: Reengineer Distribution—30% ROI   Project Completed By: December 31, 1995

Objectives	Major Tasks	Month 01	Month 02	Month 03	Month 04	Month 05	Month 06	Month 07	Month 08	Month 09	Month 10	Month 11	Month 12	Dennis	Wayne	Klaus	Dave	Owner/Priority
	1																	
	2																	
	3																	
	4																	
	5																	
	6																	
	7																	
	8																	
	9																	
	10																	
	11																	
	12																	
	13																	
	14																	
	15																	
	16																	
	17																	
	18																	
	19																	
	20																	
	21																	
	22																	
A																		
B																		
C																		
D																		
E																		

Objectives — Major Tasks — Target Dates — Costs — Summary and Forecast

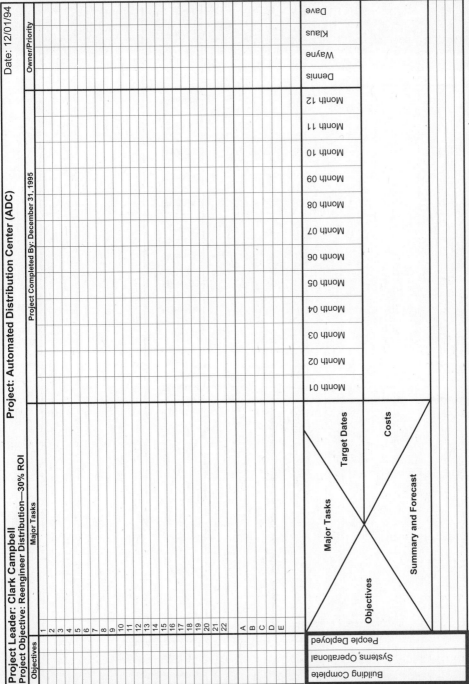

Project Leader: Clark Campbell

Project: Automated Distribution Center (ADC)

Date: 12/01/94

Project Objective: Reengineer Distribution—30% ROI

Project Completed By: December 31, 1995

Objectives	Major Tasks	Month 01	Month 02	Month 03	Month 04	Month 05	Month 06	Month 07	Month 08	Month 09	Month 10	Month 11	Month 12	Dennis	Wayne	Klaus	Dave	Owner/Priority
	1																	
	2																	
	3																	
	4																	
	5																	
	6																	
	7																	
	8																	
	9																	
	10																	
	11																	
	12																	
	13																	
	14																	
	15																	
	16																	
	17																	
	18																	
	19																	
	20																	
	21																	
	22																	
A																		
B																		
C																		
D																		
E																		

Building Complete

Systems Operational

People Deployed

Major Tasks — Target Dates

Costs

Objectives — Summary and Forecast

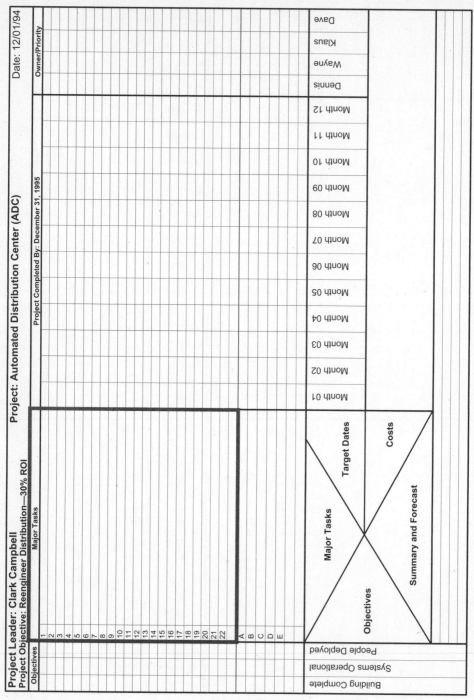

Project Leader: Clark Campbell
Project Objective: Reengineer Distribution—30% ROI

Project: Automated Distribution Center (ADC)

Date: 12/01/94

Project Completed By: December 31, 1995

Objectives

Major Tasks

Owner/Priority

Month 01
Month 02
Month 03
Month 04
Month 05
Month 06
Month 07
Month 08
Month 09
Month 10
Month 11
Month 12

Dennis
Wayne
Klaus
Dave

Major Tasks
Target Dates
Objectives
Costs
Summary and Forecast

Building Complete
Systems Operational
People Deployed

92

Project Leader: Clark Campbell **Project: Automated Distribution Center (ADC)** Date: 12/01/94

Project Objective: Reengineer Distribution—30% ROI

Project Completed By: December 31, 1995

Objectives	Major Tasks	Month 01	Month 02	Month 03	Month 04	Month 05	Month 06	Month 07	Month 08	Month 09	Month 10	Month 11	Month 12	Dennis	Wayne	Klaus	Dave
	1 Award Contracts																
	2 Site Demolition																
	3 System Software Design																
	4 Computer Hardware Specifications																
	5 Workstation Design																
	6 Parking and Landscape																
	7 Footings and Foundations																
	8 Columns and Beams																
	9 Roof Cap																
	10 Main Floor Finish																
	11 Exterior and Glass																
	12 Computer Hardware Installed																
	13 Rack Installed																
	14 Automated Cranes Installed																
	15 Conveyors Installed																
	16 Software Designed and Installed																
	17 User Training																
	18 Mezzanine Floor Finish																
	19 Work Station and Furniture																
	20 Worker Transition																
	21 Inventory Transfer																
	22 Staffing																
A																	
B																	
C																	
D																	
E																	

Building Complete · Systems Operational · People Deployed

Objectives — Major Tasks — Target Dates

Summary and Forecast — Costs

Project Leader: Clark Campbell **Project: Automated Distribution Center (ADC)** Date: 12/01/94

Project Objective: Reengineer Distribution—30% ROI

Project Completed By: December 31, 1995

Objectives

	Major Tasks	Month 01	Month 02	Month 03	Month 04	Month 05	Month 06	Month 07	Month 08	Month 09	Month 10	Month 11	Month 12	Dennis	Wayne	Klaus	Dave
1	Award Contracts																
2	Site Demolition																
3	System Software Design																
4	Computer Hardware Specifications																
5	Workstation Design																
6	Parking and Landscape																
7	Footings and Foundations																
8	Columns and Beams																
9	Roof Cap																
10	Main Floor Finish																
11	Exterior and Glass																
12	Computer Hardware Installed																
13	Rack Installed																
14	Automated Cranes Installed																
15	Conveyors Installed																
16	Software Designed and Installed																
17	User Training																
18	Mezzanine Floor Finish																
19	Work Station and Furniture																
20	Worker Transition																
21	Inventory Transfer																
22	Staffing																
A																	
B																	
C																	
D																	
E																	

Building Complete | Systems Operational | People Deployed

Major Tasks | Target Dates

Objectives | Costs

Summary and Forecast

Owner/Priority

94

Project Leader: Clark Campbell **Project: Automated Distribution Center (ADC)** Date: 12/01/94

Project Objective: Reengineer Distribution—30% ROI Project Completed By: December 31, 1995

Objectives	Major Tasks	Month 01	Month 02	Month 03	Month 04	Month 05	Month 06	Month 07	Month 08	Month 09	Month 10	Month 11	Month 12	Dennis	Wayne	Klaus	Dave
O	1 Award Contracts																
O	2 Site Demolition																
O O	3 System Software Design																
	4 Computer Hardware Specifications																
O	5 Workstation Design																
O	6 Parking and Landscape																
O	7 Footings and Foundations																
O	8 Columns and Beams																
O	9 Roof Cap																
O	10 Main Floor Finish																
O	11 Exterior and Glass																
O	12 Computer Hardware Installed																
O O	13 Rack Installed																
O	14 Automated Cranes Installed																
O	15 Conveyors Installed																
O	16 Software Designed and Installed																
O	17 User Training																
O	18 Mezzanine Floor Finish																
O	19 Work Station and Furniture																
O	20 Worker Transition																
O	21 Inventory Transfer																
O	22 Staffing																
	A																
	B																
	C																
	D																
	E																

Major Tasks

Objectives

Target Dates

Summary and Forecast

Costs

Building Complete · Systems Operational · People Deployed

Project Leader: Clark Campbell
Project: Automated Distribution Center (ADC)
Date: 12/01/94

Project Objective: Reengineer Distribution—30% ROI

Project Completed By: December 31, 1995

Objectives		Major Tasks	Owner/Priority
O	1	Award Contracts	
O	2	Site Demolition	
O	3	System Software Design	
O	4	Computer Hardware Specifications	
O	5	Workstation Design	
O	6	Parking and Landscape	
O	7	Footings and Foundations	
O	8	Columns and Beams	
O	9	Roof Cap	
O	10	Main Floor Finish	
O	11	Exterior and Glass	
O	12	Computer Hardware Installed	
O	13	Rack Installed	
O	14	Automated Cranes Installed	
O	15	Conveyors Installed	
O	16	Software Designed and Installed	
O	17	User Training	
	18	Mezzanine Floor Finish	
O	19	Work Station and Furniture	
O	20	Worker Transition	
O	21	Inventory Transfer	
O	22	Staffing	
	A		
	B		
	C		
	D		
	E		

Objectives: Building Complete | Systems Operational | People Deployed

Major Tasks — Target Dates — Costs — Summary and Forecast

Months: Month 01, Month 02, Month 03, Month 04, Month 05, Month 06, Month 07, Month 08, Month 09, Month 10, Month 11, Month 12

Owner: Dennis, Wayne, Klaus, Dave

Project Leader: Clark Campbell **Project: Automated Distribution Center (ADC)** Date: 12/01/94

Project Objective: Reengineer Distribution—30% ROI

Project Completed By: December 31, 1995

Objectives		Major Tasks	Jan-95	Feb-95	Mar-95	Apr-95	May-95	Jun-95	Jul-95	Aug-95	Sep-95	Oct-95	Nov-95	Dec-95	Dennis	Wayne	Klaus	Dave	Owner/Priority
O	1	Award Contracts																	
O	2	Site Demolition																	
O	3	System Software Design																	
	4	Computer Hardware Specifications																	
O	5	Workstation Design																	
O	6	Parking and Landscape																	
O	7	Footings and Foundations																	
O	8	Columns and Beams																	
O	9	Roof Cap																	
O	10	Main Floor Finish																	
O	11	Exterior and Glass																	
O	12	Computer Hardware Installed																	
O	13	Rack Installed																	
O	14	Automated Cranes Installed																	
O	15	Conveyors Installed																	
	16	Software Designed and Installed																	
O	17	User Training																	
O	18	Mezzanine Floor Finish																	
O	19	Work Station and Furniture																	
O	20	Worker Transition																	
O	21	Inventory Transfer																	
O	22	Staffing																	
	A																		
	B																		
	C																		
	D																		
	E																		

Building Complete — Systems Operational — People Deployed

Objectives / Major Tasks / Target Dates / Costs / Summary and Forecast

97

Project Leader: Clark Campbell | **Project: Automated Distribution Center (ADC)** | **Date: 12/01/94**

Project Objective: Reengineer Distribution—30% ROI

Project Completed By: December 31, 1995

Objectives		Major Tasks	Jan-95	Feb-95	Mar-95	Apr-95	May-95	Jun-95	Jul-95	Aug-95	Sep-95	Oct-95	Nov-95	Dec-95		Dennis	Wayne	Klaus	Dave
O	1	Award Contracts																	
O	2	Site Demolition																	
O O	3	System Software Design																	
O O	4	Computer Hardware Specifications																	
O	5	Workstation Design																	
O	6	Parking and Landscape																	
O	7	Footings and Foundations																	
O	8	Columns and Beams																	
O	9	Roof Cap																	
O	10	Main Floor Finish																	
O	11	Exterior and Glass																	
O	12	Computer Hardware Installed																	
O	13	Rack Installed																	
O	14	Automated Cranes Installed																	
O	15	Conveyors Installed																	
O	16	Software Designed and Installed																	
O	17	User Training																	
O	18	Mezzanine Floor Finish																	
O	19	Work Station and Furniture																	
O	20	Worker Transition																	
O	21	Inventory Transfer																	
O	22	Staffing																	
	A																		
	B																		
	C																		
	D																		
	E																		

Building Complete / Systems Operational / People Deployed

Target Dates — Major Tasks — Objectives

Costs — Summary and Forecast

Owner/Priority

Project Leader: Clark Campbell
Project Objective: Reengineer Distribution—30% ROI

Project: Automated Distribution Center (ADC)

Date: 12/01/94

Project Completed By: December 31, 1995

Objectives	#	Major Tasks	Jan-95	Feb-95	Mar-95	Apr-95	May-95	Jun-95	Jul-95	Aug-95	Sep-95	Oct-95	Nov-95	Dec-95	Dennis	Wayne	Klaus	Dave
O	1	Award Contracts	O	O														
O	2	Site Demolition	O	O														
O	3	System Software Design		O	O	O												
O	4	Computer Hardware Specifications		O	O													
O	5	Workstation Design			O	O	O											
O	6	Parking and Landscape				O	O	O										
O	7	Footings and Foundations		O	O	O	O											
O	8	Columns and Beams				O	O	O										
O	9	Roof Cap						O	O	O								
O	10	Main Floor Finish						O	O	O	O							
O	11	Exterior and Glass								O	O	O						
O	12	Computer Hardware Installed							O	O								
O	13	Rack Installed							O	O								
O	14	Automated Cranes Installed								O	O							
O	15	Conveyors Installed								O	O	O						
O	16	Software Designed and Installed	O				O	O	O	O	O	O	O					
O	17	User Training										O	O	O				
O	18	Mezzanine Floor Finish				O	O	O										
O	19	Work Station and Furniture									O	O	O	O				
O	20	Worker Transition										O	O					
O	21	Inventory Transfer											O	O				
O	22	Staffing		O			O				O	O	O					
	A																	
	B																	
	C																	
	D																	
	E																	

Building Complete | Systems Operational | People Deployed

Objectives — **Major Tasks** — **Target Dates**

Summary and Forecast — **Costs**

Project Leader: Clark Campbell
Project Objective: Reengineer Distribution—30% ROI
Project: Automated Distribution Center (ADC)
Date: 12/01/94

Project Completed By: December 31, 1995

#	Major Tasks	Jan-95	Feb-95	Mar-95	Apr-95	May-95	Jun-95	Jul-95	Aug-95	Sep-95	Oct-95	Nov-95	Dec-95	Dennis	Wayne	Klaus	Dave
1	Award Contracts	O	O														
2	Site Demolition	O	O														
3	System Software Design	O	O	O													
4	Computer Hardware Specifications	O	O	O	O												
5	Workstation Design			O	O												
6	Parking and Landscape				O	O	O	O									
7	Footings and Foundations		O	O	O	O	O										
8	Columns and Beams		O		O	O	O										
9	Roof Cap					O	O										
10	Main Floor Finish						O	O									
11	Exterior and Glass						O	O	O	O							
12	Computer Hardware Installed						O	O	O	O	O						
13	Rack Installed							O	O	O							
14	Automated Cranes Installed								O								
15	Conveyors Installed																
16	Software Designed and Installed					O	O	O	O	O	O	O	O				
17	User Training							O	O	O	O	O	O				
18	Mezzanine Floor Finish	O				O	O										
19	Work Station and Furniture					O	O	O	O	O	O	O					
20	Worker Transition						O	O	O		O	O					
21	Inventory Transfer					O						O					
22	Staffing		O				O				O	O	O				

Objectives: A, B, C, D, E

Objectives: Building Complete · Systems Operational · People Deployed

Owner/Priority

Major Tasks · Objectives · Target Dates · Costs · Summary and Forecast

Project Leader: Clark Campbell
Project: Automated Distribution Center (ADC) — Date: 12/01/94
Project Objective: Reengineer Distribution—30% ROI
Project Completed By: December 31, 1995

Obj.	#	Major Tasks	Jan-95	Feb-95	Mar-95	Apr-95	May-95	Jun-95	Jul-95	Aug-95	Sep-95	Oct-95	Nov-95	Dec-95	Dennis	Wayne	Klaus	Dave
O	1	Award Contracts	O												A			A
O	2	Site Demolition	O	O											A	B	A	B
O	3	System Software Design	O	O	O	O										B	A	
O	4	Computer Hardware Specifications	O	O	O												A	
O	5	Workstation Design		O	O	O	O	O							B	C		A
	6	Parking and Landscape			O	O	O								A			B
O	7	Footings and Foundations		O	O	O	O								A			
O	8	Columns and Beams				O	O	O							A			
O	9	Roof Cap						O	O	O					A	C		B
O	10	Main Floor Finish							O	O	O	O			A			C
O	11	Exterior and Glass							O	O	O	O			B	B	A	B
O	12	Computer Hardware Installed								O	O	O			B	A	B	B
O	13	Rack Installed							O	O	O	O			B	A	B	B
O	14	Automated Cranes Installed								O	O	O			B	B	A	B
O	15	Conveyors Installed									O	O	O	O	B	A	B	B
O	16	Software Designed and Installed	O			O		O		O	O	O	O	O	A	C	C	A
O	17	User Training													A			B
O	18	Mezzanine Floor Finish	O		O	O	O	O	O	O	O	O	O		B	B		B
O	19	Work Station and Furniture											O	O	B	B		A
O	20	Worker Transition											O		B	A	B	A
O	21	Inventory Transfer		O			O				O		O	O	A	B	B	B
O	22	Staffing		O											A	B		A

Objectives
A
B
C
D
E

People Deployed · Systems Operational · Building Complete

Major Tasks — Target Dates — Costs — Summary and Forecast — Objectives — Owner/Priority

Project Leader: Clark Campbell
Project Objective: Reengineer Distribution—30% ROI
Project: Automated Distribution Center (ADC)
Date: 12/01/94

Project Completed By: December 31, 1995

Obj.	#	Major Tasks	Jan-95	Feb-95	Mar-95	Apr-95	May-95	Jun-95	Jul-95	Aug-95	Sep-95	Oct-95	Nov-95	Dec-95	Dennis	Wayne	Klaus	Dave
O	1	Award Contracts	O	O											A			A
O	2	Site Demolition	O	O											A	B	B	B
O	3	System Software Design		O	O												A	A
O	4	Computer Hardware Specifications		O	O												A	B
O	5	Workstation Design		O	O	O									B	C		A
O	6	Parking and Landscape				O	O	O		O					A			B
O	7	Footings and Foundations		O	O	O		O							A			
O	8	Columns and Beams		O	O			O							A			
O	9	Roof Cap				O	O	O							A	C		B
O	10	Main Floor Finish						O	O	O					A			B
O	11	Exterior and Glass							O	O	O					B	A	C
O	12	Computer Hardware Installed						O	O	O	O				B		A	B
O	13	Rack Installed							O	O					B	A	B	B
O	14	Automated Cranes Installed								O					B	A	A	B
O	15	Conveyors Installed													B	A	B	B
O	16	Software Designed and Installed	O			O	O		O	O	O	O	O	O	A		C	B
O	17	User Training	O												B	B	A	
O	18	Mezzanine Floor Finish											O	O	A	B		A
O	19	Work Station and Furniture	O			O		O		O	O	O	O		B	B	B	B
O	20	Worker Transition											O	O	B	B		B
O	21	Inventory Transfer											O	O		B	A	A
O	22	Staffing	O				O					O		O	A	A	B	B

A	
B	
C	
D	
E	

Objectives: Building Complete · Systems Operational · People Deployed

Objectives | Major Tasks | Target Dates | Costs

Summary and Forecast

Project: Automated Distribution Center (ADC)

Date: 12/01/94

Project Leader: Clark Campbell
Project Objective: Reengineer Distribution—30% ROI

Project Completed By: December 31, 1995

#	Major Tasks	Building Complete	Systems Operational	People Deployed	Jan-95	Feb-95	Mar-95	Apr-95	May-95	Jun-95	Jul-95	Aug-95	Sep-95	Oct-95	Nov-95	Dec-95	Dennis	Wayne	Klaus	Dave
1	Award Contracts	O			O	O											A			
2	Site Demolition	O			O	O											A	B	A	B
3	System Software Design		O		O	O	O											B	A	B
4	Computer Hardware Specifications		O		O	O	O											C		A
5	Workstation Design			O		O	O	O	O	O							B			
6	Parking and Landscape	O						O	O	O	O						A	C		B
7	Footings and Foundations	O						O	O								A			
8	Columns and Beams	O						O	O								A			
9	Roof Cap	O							O	O	O						A	C		B
10	Main Floor Finish	O							O	O	O						A	B	B	C
11	Exterior and Glass	O								O	O						B	A	C	
12	Computer Hardware Installed	O									O	O					B	A	B	B
13	Rack Installed	O									O	O					B	B	A	B
14	Automated Cranes Installed	O															B	A	B	B
15	Conveyors Installed	O												O	O		A	A	C	B
16	Software Designed and Installed	O			O			O	O	O	O	O	O	O			B			B
17	User Training	O															B		A	
18	Mezzanine Floor Finish				O			O	O	O	O	O	O	O			A	B	B	B
19	Work Station and Furniture											O	O	O			B	B	A	B
20	Worker Transition	O											O	O				B		A
21	Inventory Transfer	O										O	O	O			A		B	B
22	Staffing	O				O			O			O					B			B

	Objectives	Building Complete	Systems Operational	People Deployed													Dennis	Wayne	Klaus	Dave
A	Internal Software Operational		O	O														B	A	B
B	External Software Operational		O	O														B	A	A
C	Integration Software Operational		O															B	A	B
D	Full Consolidation Operational	O	O	O																A
E	Go Live on Time	O	O	O													A	A	A	A

Target Dates — Costs

Major Tasks — Objectives

Summary and Forecast

Owner/Priority

Project Leader: Clark Campbell
Project Objective: Reengineer Distribution—30% ROI

Project: Automated Distribution Center (ADC)
Date: 12/01/94

Project Completed By: December 31, 1995

Objectives	#	Major Tasks	Jan-95	Feb-95	Mar-95	Apr-95	May-95	Jun-95	Jul-95	Aug-95	Sep-95	Oct-95	Nov-95	Dec-95	Dennis	Wayne	Klaus	Dave
O	1	Award Contracts	O	O											A			A
O	2	Site Demolition	O	O											A	B		B
O	3	System Software Design	O	O	O	O											A	A
O	4	Computer Hardware Specifications	O	O	O	O										B	A	B
O	5	Workstation Design			O	O												
	6	Parking and Landscape					O	O							B			
	7	Footings and Foundations			O		O	O	O	O					A	C		
	8	Columns and Beams				O	O	O							A			A
	9	Roof Cap					O	O							A			B
O	10	Main Floor Finish						O	O	O	O				A	C		
O	11	Exterior and Glass						O	O	O					A			B
O	12	Computer Hardware Installed									O	O			B	B	A	C
O	13	Rack Installed								O	O				B	A	A	B
O	14	Automated Cranes Installed							O	O	O	O			B	A	B	B
O	15	Conveyors Installed							O	O	O	O			B		A	B
O	16	Software Designed and Installed	O			O	O	O	O	O	O	O	O		B	B	C	A
O	17	User Training												O	A			B
	18	Mezzanine Floor Finish													B		A	A
O	19	Work Station and Furniture	O	O			O	O	O	O		O	O		A	B		B
O	20	Worker Transition	O										O	O	B	B		A
O	21	Inventory Transfer	O										O	O	B	A	B	B
O	22	Staffing		O												B	A	A

		Objectives	Jan-95	Feb-95	Mar-95	Apr-95	May-95	Jun-95	Jul-95	Aug-95	Sep-95	Oct-95	Nov-95	Dec-95	Dennis	Wayne	Klaus	Dave
O	A	Internal Software Operational															A	B
O	B	External Software Operational													B	B	A	A
O	C	Integration Software Operational													B	A	A	B
O	D	Full Consolidation Operational													A	A	A	A
O	E	Go Live on Time													A	B		A

Bottom objective summary rows: **People Deployed** · **Systems Operational** · **Building Complete**

Central panels: **Major Tasks** · **Target Dates** · **Costs** · **Objectives** · **Summary and Forecast**

Owner/Priority

Project Leader: Clark Campbell **Project: Automated Distribution Center (ADC)** **Date: 12/01/94**

Project Objective: Reengineer Distribution—30% ROI

Project Completed By: December 31, 1995

#	Major Tasks	Jan-95	Feb-95	Mar-95	Apr-95	May-95	Jun-95	Jul-95	Aug-95	Sep-95	Oct-95	Nov-95	Dec-95	Dennis	Wayne	Klaus	Dave
1	Award Contracts	O	O											A			A
2	Site Demolition	O	O											A	B	A	B
3	System Software Design	O	O	O	O										B	A	A
4	Computer Hardware Specifications	O	O	O										B	C		A
5	Workstation Design			O	O									A			B
6	Parking and Landscape					O	O	O	O					A			
7	Footings and Foundations		O	O	O	O								A			
8	Columns and Beams					O	O							A			
9	Roof Cap						O	O	O	O				A	C		B
10	Main Floor Finish						O	O	O	O				A			B
11	Exterior and Glass							O	O	O	O				B	A	C
12	Computer Hardware Installed								O	O	O	O		B	A	B	B
13	Rack Installed							O	O	O	O			B		A	B
14	Automated Cranes Installed								O	O	O			B	A	A	B
15	Conveyors Installed										O	O	O		B		B
16	Software Designed and Installed	O	O	O	O	O	O								B	C	B
17	User Training											O	O	A	B	B	B
18	Mezzanine Floor Finish	O	O	O	O	O	O							B	B	B	A
19	Work Station and Furniture										O	O	O	B	B		A
20	Worker Transition									O	O	O			A	B	B
21	Inventory Transfer									O	O	O	O		B	B	A
22	Staffing		O		O		O		O	O	O				B	B	A

Objectives

	Objectives	People Deployed	Systems Operational	Building Complete
A	Internal Software Operational	O	O	
B	External Software Operational	O	O	
C	Integration Software Operational	O	O	
D	Full Consolidation Operational	O	O	
E	Go Live on Time	O	O	O

Summary and Forecast

Costs
- Building $6.0 million
- System $3.0 million
- People $0.5 million

(Target Dates / Major Tasks)

Project Leader: Clark Campbell — **Project: Automated Distribution Center (ADC)** — **Date: 12/01/94**

Project Objective: Reengineer Distribution—30% ROI

Project Completed By: December 31, 1995

Objectives:
- A Internal Software Operational
- B External Software Operational
- C Integration Software Operational
- D Full Consolidation Operational
- E Go Live on Time

Objectives columns: People Deployed / Systems Operational / Building Complete

#	Major Tasks	Target Dates (Jan-95 … Dec-95)	Dennis	Wayne	Klaus	Dave
1	Award Contracts	Jan–Feb 95	A			A
2	Site Demolition	Jan–Feb 95	A	B		A
3	System Software Design	Feb–Apr 95		B	A	B
4	Computer Hardware Specifications	Feb–Mar 95		B	A	A
5	Workstation Design	Feb–Mar 95	B	C		A
6	Parking and Landscape	Apr–Jun 95	A	A		B
7	Footings and Foundations	Apr–May 95	A			
8	Columns and Beams	Apr–May 95	A			
9	Roof Cap	May–Jun 95	A			
10	Main Floor Finish	Jun–Jul 95	A	C		B
11	Exterior and Glass	Jun–Jul 95	A			B
12	Computer Hardware Installed	Aug 95		B	A	C
13	Rack Installed	Jul–Aug 95	B	A	B	B
14	Automated Cranes Installed	Jul–Aug 95	B	A	A	B
15	Conveyors Installed	Aug–Sep 95	B	A	B	B
16	Software Designed and Installed	Jan–Oct 95	B	B	A	B
17	User Training	Nov–Dec 95		A	C	C
18	Mezzanine Floor Finish	Jun–Aug 95	A	B		B
19	Work Station and Furniture	Sep–Nov 95	B	B	B	A
20	Worker Transition	Nov–Dec 95		B	B	A
21	Inventory Transfer	Oct–Dec 95		A	A	B
22	Staffing	Feb–Dec 95		B	B	A

Costs:
- People $0.5 million
- System $3.0 million
- Building $6.0 million

Summary and Forecast

Project Leader: Clark Campbell **Project: Automated Distribution Center (ADC)** Date: 12/01/94

Project Objective: Reengineer Distribution—30% ROI

Project Completed By: December 31, 1995

Objectives (Building Complete / Systems Operational / People Deployed)	#	Major Tasks	Jan-95	Feb-95	Mar-95	Apr-95	May-95	Jun-95	Jul-95	Aug-95	Sep-95	Oct-95	Nov-95	Dec-95	Dennis	Wayne	Klaus	Dave
	1	Award Contracts	O	O											A	B		
	2	Site Demolition	O	O											A	B	A	B
	3	System Software Design	O	O	O											B	A	A
	4	Computer Hardware Specifications	O	O	O													A
	5	Workstation Design			O	O									B	C		
	6	Parking and Landscape				O	O								A			A
	7	Footings and Foundations		O	O	O									A			B
	8	Columns and Beams			O	O									A			
	9	Roof Cap					O	O							A			
	10	Main Floor Finish					O	O	O						A	C		B
	11	Exterior and Glass						O	O						A			C
	12	Computer Hardware Installed								O	O				B	B	A	B
	13	Rack Installed							O	O					B	A	B	B
	14	Automated Cranes Installed								O					B	A	B	B
	15	Conveyors Installed									O	O				B	B	B
	16	Software Designed and Installed	O	O						O	O	O	O	O		B	C	B
	17	User Training												O	A	B	A	C
	18	Mezzanine Floor Finish	O	O						O	O		O	O	B	B		A
	19	Work Station and Furniture											O			B	B	B
	20	Worker Transition								O	O	O	O			A	A	A
	21	Inventory Transfer		O			O						O			B	B	B
	22	Staffing									O	O			A	B	A	A

Objectives
A Internal Software Operational
B External Software Operational
C Integration Software Operational
D Full Consolidation Operational
E Go Live on Time

Major Tasks / Target Dates / Objectives / Costs / Summary and Forecast

Costs: People $0.5 million — System $3.0 million — Building $6.0 million

The ADC Project is scheduled to start January 1, 1995 and be completed by December 31, 1995. It will cost $10 million and will deliver an initial ROI of 30%.

The One-Page Project Manager in Action

Before showing you how the One-Page Project Manager (OPPM) was used during the year our Automated Distribution Center (ADC) project took, I think it worthwhile for you to see the version (see Figure 6.1) we developed before the project began. This was a very important iteration because this version was used to gain upper management's final approval to start the project.

FIVE STEPS TO CREATING A REPORT USING THE ONE-PAGE PROJECT MANAGER

We are now ready to use our freshly built One-Page Project Manager. The careful work and team building

Project Leader: Clark Campbell	Project: Automated Distribution Center (ADC)	Date: 12/01/94
Project Objective: Reengineer Distribution—30% ROI		

Project Completed By: December 31, 1995

Objectives	#	Major Tasks	Owner/Priority (Dennis / Wayne / Klaus / Dave)
	1	Award Contracts	A
	2	Site Demolition	A, B
	3	System Software Design	B, A, B
	4	Computer Hardware Specifications	A
	5	Workstation Design	B, C, A
	6	Parking and Landscape	A, B
	7	Footings and Foundations	A
	8	Columns and Beams	A
	9	Roof Cap	A
	10	Main Floor Finish	A, C, B
	11	Exterior and Glass	A, B
	12	Computer Hardware Installed	B, A, C
	13	Rack Installed	B, A, B
	14	Automated Cranes Installed	B, A, B, B
	15	Conveyors Installed	B, A, B, B
	16	Software Designed and Installed	B, A, B, B
	17	User Training	A, C, B
	18	Mezzanine Floor Finish	A, B, B
	19	Work Station and Furniture	B, B, A
	20	Worker Transition	B, A
	21	Inventory Transfer	A, B, B
	22	Staffing	B, A
	A	Internal Software Operational	A, B
	B	External Software Operational	B, A
	C	Integration Software Operational	B, A, B
	D	Full Consolidation Operational	B, A, B
	E	Go Live on Time	A, A, A, A

Objectives (left axis): Building Complete, Systems Operational, People Deployed

Major Tasks / Target Dates / Objectives / Costs / Summary and Forecast

Target Dates (months): Jan-95, Feb-95, Mar-95, Apr-95, May-95, Jun-95, Jul-95, Aug-95, Sep-95, Oct-95, Nov-95, Dec-95

Owners: Dennis, Wayne, Klaus, Dave

Costs: Building $6.0 million · System $3.0 million · People $0.5 million

The ADC Project is scheduled to start January 1, 1995 and be completed by December 31, 1995. It will cost $10 million and will deliver an initial ROI of 30%.

FIGURE 6.1   *The One-Page Project Manager at the start of the ADC project.*

Copyright O.C. Tanner 2007. **To customize this document, download it to your hard drive from the following web site: www.onepageprojectmanager.com.** The document can be opened, edited, and printed using Microsoft Excel or another popular spreadsheet application.

required to construct your One-Page Project Manager now pays off. Monthly reports are easy when you follow the five steps in Figure 6.2 on page 111.

You meet with your project's owners near the conclusion of each Target Date and complete the following tasks:

1. *Bold the Target Date.*
2. *Fill in Major Task progress.* Designate the project's progress by filling in the dots. While filling in the dots is easy, getting agreement on which to fill in, or not fill in, is often anything but easy. Some team members will say, "Yes, fill in my dot," and others

ers may say, "That's not done yet." Your job as project manager is to bring the team together. This requires straight talk—very direct, unambiguous communication. Very important: Once you decide which dots to fill in and which not to, the team has to agree. Once the One-Page Project Manager is completed, you can't have a team member say that the report is not quite accurate, is not candid—or that the team is being anything less than honest. If this happens, the efficacy and credibility of the One-Page Project Manager is undermined. The project team absolutely must be unified, and the team leader must work with team members until they

Project Leader: Clark Campbell	Project: Automated Distribution Center (ADC)	Date: 03/31/95
Project Objective: Reengineer Distribution—30% ROI		

#	Major Tasks	Project Completed By: December 31, 1995	Owner/Priority
1	Award Contracts		A
2	Site Demolition		A B
3	System Software Design		B A B
4	Computer Hardware Specifications		A
5	Workstation Design		B C A
6	Parking and Landscape		A B
7	Footings and Foundations		A
8	Columns and Beams		A
9	Roof Cap		A
10	Main Floor Finish		A C B
11	Exterior and Glass		A B
12	Computer Hardware Installed		B A C
13	Rack Installed		B A B
14	Automated Cranes Installed		B A B B
15	Conveyors Installed		B A B B
16	Software Designed and Installed		B A B
17	User Training		A C B
18	Mezzanine Floor Finish		A B B
19	Work Station and Furniture		B B A
20	Worker Transition		B A
21	Inventory Transfer		A B B
22	Staffing		B A
A	Internal Software Operational		A B
B	External Software Operational		B A
C	Integration Software Operational		B A
D	Full Consolidation Operational		B A B
E	Go Live on Time		A A A A

Objectives: Building Complete · Systems Operational · People Deployed

Target Dates (Months): Jan-95, Feb-95, Mar-95, Apr-95, May-95, Jun-95, Jul-95, Aug-95, Sep-95, Oct-95, Nov-95, Dec-95

Owners: Dennis, Wayne, Klaus, Dave

Costs: Building $6.0 million · System $3.0 million · People $0.5 million

Green = · Yellow = · Red =

Summary and Forecast: The integration of new software with current systems is proving more complex than expected. The modest cost overruns are expected to be recovered. Building change orders are being kept to a minimum. The transition team leaders have been identified and are now involved. We continue on-track to meet our timing, budget, and ROI objectives.

FIGURE 6.2   **Five steps in building monthly reports.**

Copyright O.C. Tanner 2007. To customize this document, download it to your hard drive from the following web site: www.onepageprojectmanager.com. The document can be opened, edited, and printed using Microsoft Excel or another popular spreadsheet application.

Only then, should the One-Page Project Manager be signed and submitted to upper management.

3. *Designate qualitative performance.* Use colors when designating qualitative performance. As with most things in life, color choices are not limited to black and white (pun intended). Before you start the project, clearly define what each color means. The project leader does this in conjunction with team members. You and your team may have your own definitions of the colors, and they may vary a bit from project to project. Here is how we usually define them at O.C. Tanner:

- *Green: Adequate performance*—Performance is good enough. (We do not acknowledge superior performance with colors; what's important is to let management know when things are progressing adequately.)

- *Yellow: Worrisome performance*—Performance may affect the timing, scope, or cost of the project. Problems designated with yellow are expected by the task's owner to be transient and solvable.

- *Red: Dangerous performance*—Performance will affect the timing, scope, or budget of the project. For these tasks to be resolved, efforts beyond those of the individual task owner will be required.
A team effort is needed to resolve these problems.

4. *Report expenditures:* Figures should come from the accounting department, which has to be in agreement with how the budget is portrayed on the One-Page Project Manager. Actual expenditures are shown as a bar juxtaposed to the budget. This gives a

clear picture of the amount of the budget spent to date, and whether you are spending above, under, or on budget. Again, colors are used:

- *Green:* Project is on or under budget.
- *Yellow:* Project is over budget, but either expect to find savings to eventually return to budget, or you are within a previously agreed to contingency percentage.
- *Red:* Project is over budget and you expect to end the project over budget and over any previously approved contingency percentage.

5. *Write the Summary and Forecast.*

EXAMPLES OF THE ONE-PAGE PROJECT MANAGER IN ACTION

The blue vertical line is where we are today. The circles show where each task is on the timeline.

Figures 6.3 through Figure 6.6 show how the One-Page Project Manager changes over time as a project progresses. The One-Page Project Managers being used are from a project I managed—the building of O.C. Tanner's Automated Distribution Center (ADC). The project began in January of 1995 and ended in December of that year, exactly correlating with the calendar year. I've chosen 3 months in the life of this 12-month project to highlight these action illustrations.

The One-Page Project Manager should be completed in a timely manner. If it is weeks late, it is largely useless. If the time allotments used are monthly, then the tool should be completed within five working days of the end of each month. Don't procrastinate. Fill in the One-Page Project Manager as soon as you can.

When completing the One-Page Project Manager, you and your team (the owners) finalize what to do then open up the discussion to your broader team, the others involved with the project. Ask them if they think the One-Page Project Manager you and team have created accurately represents where the project is currently. This helps engage a wide group of interested parties, it brings in new ideas and—very important—it helps maintain the honesty and integrity of the owners. When they know that others will judge their decisions, they become more likely to be realistic with their claims. They may want to say that a certain task is on time, for example, but knowing that others involved with the task will have an opportunity to comment, the owners may change their minds and say the task is somewhat behind schedule.

A Report Early in the Project

The blue line on Figure 6.3 tells you where in the life span of the project you are. Figure 6.3 has the blue line at March 1995, telling you this One-Page Project Manager was compiled as of the March 1995 report, which was three months into the project. You can see a number of black dots related to tasks.

The first two tasks, Award Contracts (line 1) and Site Demolition (line 2), were supposed to be completed within the first two months of the project. Looking at Figure 6.3, you don't know when they were completed, but you know they are finished at this time; the previous One-Page Project Manager, for

Project Leader: Clark Campbell Project Objective: Reengineer Distribution—30% ROI		Project: Automated Distribution Center (ADC)														Date: 03/31/95			
Objectives	#	Major Tasks	Project Completed By: December 31, 1995													Owner/Priority			
			Jan-95	Feb-95	Mar-95	Apr-95	May-95	Jun-95	Jul-95	Aug-95	Sep-95	Oct-95	Nov-95	Dec-95	Dennis	Wayne	Klaus	Dave
●	1	Award Contracts	●	●											A			
●	2	Site Demolition	●	●											A	B		
O	3	System Software Design	●	●	●	○									B	A		B
O	4	Computer Hardware Specifications	●	●	○											A		
O	5	Workstation Design		●	●	●									B	C		A
O	6	Parking and Landscape					○	○							A			B
O	7	Footings and Foundations		●	●	○	○								A			
O	8	Columns and Beams				○	○	○							A			
O	9	Roof Cap					○	○	○						A			
O	10	Main Floor Finish					○	○	○	○	○				A	C		B
O	11	Exterior and Glass					○	○	○	○	○	○			A			B
O	12	Computer Hardware Installed							○	○	○				B	A	C	
O O	13	Rack Installed						○	○						B	A		B
O O	14	Automated Cranes Installed						○	○						B	A	B	B
O O	15	Conveyors Installed							○	○	○				B	A	B	B
O	16	Software Designed and Installed	●	●	●	○	○	○	○	○	○	○	○		A	B		B
O	17	User Training								○	○	○	○	○	A	C		B
O	18	Mezzanine Floor Finish						○	○	○	○	○			A	B		B
O	19	Work Station and Furniture	●	●	●	●	○	○	○	○	○	○			B	B		A
O	20	Worker Transition										○			B			A
O	21	Inventory Transfer										○	○		A	B	B	
O	22	Staffing	●			○					○	○	○		B			A
O	A	Internal Software Operational														A		B
O	B	External Software Operational													B	A		
O	C	Integration Software Operational													B	A		B
O O O	D	Full Consolidation Operational													B	A		B
O O O	E	Go Live on Time													A	A	A	A

Objectives (left axis): Building Complete · Systems Operational · People Deployed

Summary and Forecast — Major Tasks / Target Dates / Objectives / Costs

Costs:
- Building $6.0 million
- $2.1 million
- System $3.0 million
- $0.9 million
- People $0.5 million

Legend: Green = / Yellow = / Red =

The integration of new software with current systems is proving more complex than expected. The modest cost overruns are expected to be recovered. Building change orders are being kept to a minimum. The transition team leaders have been identified and are now involved. We continue on-track to meet our timing, budget, and ROI objectives.

FIGURE 6.3 *The March 1995 Report.*

February, would have told you if the tasks were completed exactly on time. The third task, System Software Design (line 3), is on time because all the dots up to the present are black. The fourth task, Computer Hardware Specifications (line 4), is behind schedule (there is an empty circle in March). The next task, Workstation Design (line 5) is ahead of schedule (there is a black circle to the right of the blue line, in the April column). Notice how easily and quickly a reader can ascertain which tasks are on time, ahead of schedule or behind, and which are currently completed.

115

When you look at Subjective Tasks (lines A through E), you will see bar graphs alongside them. In the March 1995 illustration, Internal Software Operational (line A) and Go Live on Time (line E) both have green lines for the entire length of the project up to the present (March). The green says these Subjective Tasks are performing adequately. Two tasks don't have any lines— Integration Software Operational (line C) and Full Consolidation Operational (line D) because they have yet to be started. One task, External Software Operational (line B) has a yellow line beginning in the second month (February) and continuing into March. This means this task began in February and, because the line is yellow, performance is troublesome.

The One-Page Project Manager also connects tasks to Objectives. Notice that the first two tasks, Award Contracts (line 1) and Site Demolition (line 2) have their circles on the timeline filled in, indicating they are finished. Note that the Objectives connected to these tasks (Building Complete) also have black circles. That's because the tasks connected to this objective have been completed. As you look at Figures 6.4 and 6.5, you see that as tasks are completed, Objectives are checked off.

The mechanism for this is quite simple. As a task is completed, the circle(s) aligned with the Objective(s) is filled in. Over time, the One-Page Project Manager quickly lets observers see which Objectives have been fulfilled and which still need work.

Budget and Costs

You can see in Figure 6.3 how the budget line progresses. The Building budget is a green line at $2.1 million. This means that at this point, $2.1 million of the $6.0 million Building budget has been spent, and that this portion of the project is on budget (the green indicates it is on budget). Of the system's $3.0 million budget, $0.9 has been spent. This line is yellow, which tells management that this portion of the project is over budget, yet recoverable. The People portion is quite small and we haven't specified how much of it has been spent at this time, but the bar graph shows just a small amount has been spent on People and that this portion of the budget gets a green line, which indicates all is well.

Summary and Forecast

The integration of new software with current systems is proving more complex than expected [the why]. The modest cost overruns are expected to be recovered [what you expect will happen].

A Report Midway through the Project

Again, the essence of the One-Page Project Manager is comprehended quickly by reading in a circle (see Figure 6.4)—from Objectives to Tasks to the Target Dates and timeline to Owners to Costs to Summary and Forecast. The illustration for July 1995 (see Figure 6.5) shows more dots filled in, which is what you would expect as a project progresses. Notice how many tasks are now behind schedule. Parking and Landscaping (line 6) has two empty circles and is therefore two months behind. The comment in the Summary and Forecast at the bottom of the page explains this lateness: "Heavy rains and mud have delayed construction [the why]." "Plans are in place to catch up [what you are doing about it and what you expect will happen]." Other late tasks include

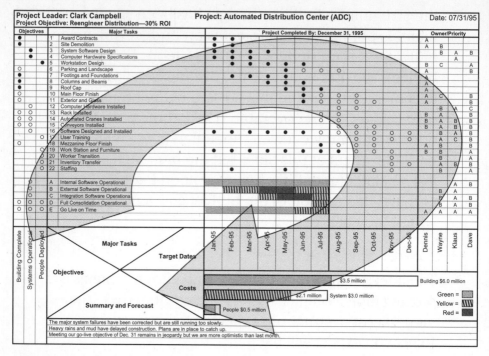

FIGURE 6.4   *Read OPPM's in a circle.*

Copyright O.C. Tanner 2007. **To customize this document, download it to your hard drive from the following web site: www.onepageprojectmanager.com.** The document can be opened, edited, and printed using Microsoft Excel or another popular spreadsheet application.

Main Floor Finish (line 10), Exterior and Glass (line 11), Rack Installed (line 13), Automated Cranes Installed (line 14), and Software Designed and Installed (line 16).

You don't want to sugarcoat or gloss over potential problems. You want to be honest and forthright, but still positive. The summary states: "Meeting our go-live objective of Dec. 31 remains in jeopardy but we are more optimistic than last month." This is an honest assessment of the situation. The project was in jeopardy of not being completed on time, yet the situation had improved enough that the project team was feeling more optimistic about meeting the ultimate deadline (in fact, it was met).

Project Leader: Clark Campbell		Project: Automated Distribution Center (ADC)	Date: 07/31/95
Project Objective: Reengineer Distribution—30% ROI			

Figure contents (One-Page Project Manager grid):

Objectives / Major Tasks (Project Completed By: December 31, 1995) / Owner-Priority

#	Major Tasks	Owner/Priority
1	Award Contracts	A
2	Site Demolition	A B
3	System Software Design	B A B
4	Computer Hardware Specifications	A
5	Workstation Design	B C A
6	Parking and Landscape	A B
7	Footings and Foundations	A
8	Columns and Beams	A
9	Roof Cap	A
10	Main Floor Finish	A C B
11	Exterior and Glass	A B
12	Computer Hardware Installed	B A C
13	Rack Installed	B A B
14	Automated Cranes Installed	B A B B
15	Conveyors Installed	B A B B
16	Software Designed and Installed	B A B
17	User Training	A C B
18	Mezzanine Floor Finish	A B B
19	Work Station and Furniture	B B A
20	Worker Transition	B
21	Inventory Transfer	A B B
22	Staffing	B A
A	Internal Software Operational	A B
B	External Software Operational	B A
C	Integration Software Operational	B A B
D	Full Consolidation Operational	B A B
E	Go Live on Time	A A A A

Timeline months: Jan-95, Feb-95, Mar-95, Apr-95, May-95, Jun-95, Jul-95, Aug-95, Sep-95, Oct-95, Nov-95, Dec-95
Owners: Dennis, Wayne, Klaus, Dave

Left axis objectives: Building Complete, Systems Operational, People Deployed

Diagram center labels: Major Tasks / Target Dates / Objectives / Costs / Summary and Forecast

Costs:
- Building $6.0 million ($3.5 million)
- System $3.0 million ($2.1 million)
- People $0.5 million
- Green = / Yellow = / Red =

Summary and Forecast:
The major system failures have been corrected but are still running too slowly.
Heavy rains and mud have delayed construction. Plans are in place to catch up.
Meeting our go-live objective of Dec. 31 remains in jeopardy but we are more optimistic than last month.

FIGURE 6.5 *The July 1995 Report.*

Tasks now completed include Award Contracts (line 1), Site Demolition (line 2), System Software Design (line 3), Computer Hardware Specifications (line 4), and Workstation Design (line 5). Also completed are Footings and Foundations (line 7), Columns and Beams (line 8), and Roof Cap (line 9).

Other tasks have not yet begun. You can tell when they are due to start by the month in which the first circle is located. For example, Computer Hardware Installed (line 12) will start in August 1995, User Training (line 17) will start in September, Worker Transition (line 20) begins and ends in November, as does Inventory Transfer (line 21).

119

Under Subjective Tasks, Figure 6.4 indicates that Internal Software Operational (line A) has been adequately operating for the entire project. Go Live on Time (line E) was, for the first five months, green, but circumstances have put the project's final deadline in jeopardy and that's why it's had yellow for the past two months. Both External Software Operational (line B) and Integration Software Operational (line C) are now yellow, meaning that they are having recoverable performance issues. Previously, they each had two months of red, which meant those tasks were so dysfunctional that they jeopardized the entire project.

Budget and Costs

Since Figure 6.3, the Building budget graph has moved right, indicating $3.5 million has been spent. It still is green, which says all is well. The System budget has spent $2.1 million, and its yellow line shows that this portion of the overall budget remains more costly than expected. The People budget has been more than 50 percent consumed (the line is more than halfway filled in), and because the line is green, it remains on budget.

The Summary & Forecast section addresses explanations for late tasks, system challenges, and budget over runs, while giving a studied look into the near future. Some optimism is reflected in both the language and the graphics, especially given the two previous month's reports.

A Report near the End of the Project

In Figure 6.6, all the tasks were due to be completed but three. Two of these three were completed early—User

Project Leader: Clark Campbell Project Objective: Reengineer Distribution—30% ROI	Project: Automated Distribution Center (ADC)	Date: 11/30/95	Owner/Priority
Objectives	Major Tasks	Project Completed By: December 31, 1995	
•	1 Award Contracts		A
•	2 Site Demolition		A B
	3 System Software Design		B A B
	4 Computer Hardware Specifications		A
	5 Workstation Design		B C A
•	6 Parking and Landscape		A B
•	7 Footings and Foundations		A
•	8 Columns and Beams		A
•	9 Roof Cap		A
•	10 Main Floor Finish		A C B
•	11 Exterior and Glass		A B
	12 Computer Hardware Installed		B A C
	13 Rack Installed		B A B
	14 Automated Cranes Installed		B A B
	15 Conveyors Installed		B A B
○	16 Software Designed and Installed		A C B
	17 User Training		A A C B
•	18 Mezzanine Floor Finish		A B B
	19 Work Station and Furniture		B B A
	20 Worker Transition		B A
	21 Inventory Transfer		A B B
	22 Staffing		B A
			A B
•	A Internal Software Operational		B A
○	B External Software Operational		B A B
•	C Integration Software Operational		B A B
○ ○ ○	D Full Consolidation Operational		B A B
○ ○ ○	E Go Live on Time		A A A A

Building Complete / Systems Operational / People Deployed

Major Tasks — Target Dates — Jan-95, Feb-95, Mar-95, Apr-95, May-95, Jun-95, Jul-95, Aug-95, Sep-95, Oct-95, Nov-95, Dec-95 — Dennis, Wayne, Klaus, Dave

Objectives — Costs

Summary and Forecast

$5.3m   Building $6.0 million
System $3.0 million
$3.2m
People $0.5 million

Green =
Yellow =
Red =

Project will be completed on time.
System cost overruns are more than offset by savings secured in the construction process.
We are confident that the remaining software issues will be resolved and adequate for go-live. Refinements will still be required.
People have been trained, and are anxious to begin full operation.

FIGURE 6.6   *The November 1995 Report.*

Training (line 17) and Inventory Transfer (line 21)—and Software Designed and Installed (line 16) is on schedule and planned for completion next month.

Three Subjective Tasks are working well (those in green) but two tasks are still troublesome. Look closely at the Objectives aligned with the Subjective Tasks. Two Subjective Tasks—Internal Software Operational (line A) and Integration Software Operational (line C)—have circles for their Objectives filled in, indicating the Objectives associated with these tasks are complete. But the other three tasks still have Objectives outstanding. Go Live on Time (line E) has a green line. It is important to note that the two

121

remaining subjective tasks, External Software Operational (line B) and Full Consolidation Operational (line D) have yellow lines and still show symptoms of sluggish performance—but are not poor enough to cause a delay in the Go Live on Time task.

Budget and Costs

The Building budget has used $5.3 million of the $6.0 allotted to it, and it is green, so it is on budget. The System budget remains in trouble. It is yellow, with a portion in red. That tells us that the System budget has spent more than was budgeted. The yellow has been saying for months that this portion of the project was spending more than expected, and the red says that the spending has now exceeded the budget. You can see how much over budget the System budget is by looking at the $3.2 million figure in the bar graph and the $3.0 million allocated to this in the budget. With still a month left to the project, the System portion of the project has gone $200,000 over budget. The People budget is still green and has nearly filled its bar graph, showing that almost all of the $500,000 allocated to people has been spent.

Summary and Forecast

The summary states, "Project will be completed on time." That lets management know where the project stands. The summary also says, "System cost overruns are more than offset by savings secured in the construction process." This tells management that now, near the very end of the project, savings in the construction side of the project will offset the cost overruns that have been seen for months with the System. The software systems issues are much improved and now "adequate for go-live." However, "refinements to the system will still be required" following start-up.

MEETINGS ARE BETTER WITH THE ONE-PAGE PROJECT MANAGER

Using the One-Page Project Manager provides numerous benefits, including:

- Every project meeting, from general management to project team meetings, is shorter, more efficient, and more effective.
- The agenda for each meeting relating to each project is essentially the same. That's because the *agenda* is the One-Page Project Manager.
- Each participant becomes very familiar with the One-Page Project Manager and how it works because it is used ubiquitously within the organization.
- Everyone at every meeting knows what will be discussed and what he or she will need to report on, and can therefore come prepared.
- Less time is spent at meetings and more time is spent running the project.
- Communication to all interested parties is simple—they can each get a copy of the One-Page Project Manager. You can't readily send Microsoft Project or Primavera P3 (project management software products) to the board of directors or other stakeholders, but you can send the One-Page Project Manager to all of them.
- The simplicity and directness of the One-Page Project Manager drives efficiency and straight talk.

Variations of the One-Page Project Manager

The One-Page Project Manager templates for the following projects may be viewed on the Internet at www.onepageprojectmanager.com.

ISO IMPLEMENTATION

On the left side of the One-Page Project Manager for the ISO implementation project, there is a list of major tasks that fits into our general model. But to the left of these, we've divided the tasks into four phases—Definition Phase, Implementation Phase, Verification Phase, and Validation. We did this to make the progress of the project easier to grasp. This particular project lent itself to being divided into phases. Not all projects do, but I recommend you use this tactic if your project has distinct phases.

Since this project was to be judged by a third party—BSI Management Systems, the organization that monitors ISO credentials—it has timelines that highlight when we would be audited—Pre-Audit Assessment (October 22 to 24) and Registration Audit (November 17 to 21). These were important deadlines and ones we could not easily control, which is why they are so prominently highlighted.

On the budget lines, which are near the bottom, we list Consultant Costs and Registrar Costs. Again, this had to do with the fact that a third party was involved. The Registrar Costs are set by the credentialing organization, and are not variable. For this reason, we segregated the Registrar Costs from the Consultant Costs, which are variable.

Below the budget is Documents. This is the paperwork—the documentation of how you do things. They are the essence of ISO certification and are required to gain certification. Those supervising the certification process use your documentation to assess what you say you will do, if you do it, and how you know.

In the lower right, where the owners are listed, we associated a subtask to each owner. We went into such detail because this project had more subtasks than most, and it was important that each subtask be delineated and that each subtask had its owner on the one-page project manager.

ENTRADA

Entrada was a new dot-com business we created. This particular variation of the One-Page Project Manager has much in common with the standard format, but there are some significant differences.

At the upper left-hand corner, we list Prospects, with various customers in this section that we were trying to win. It was critical that we monitor our progress on signing up new customers on a customer-by-customer basis.

To the right of the customers, the senior vice presidents (SVPs) who "owned" these customers are listed as well as Travel in 2 Weeks (whether the owners will be traveling during the next two weeks).

Below Prospects is a section devoted to Current Customers—companies that we had won and that were now our customers. This was a new business we were launching, and this one-page project manager is designed to support that by keeping an eye on the infrastructure needed to support and expand the business, following the sales process for landing new customers, and noting which new customers had come onboard. The usual task format is included on the figure to drive completion of the project task necessary to build the new business systems and processes.

FINISHING CORNERSTONE

This was a major ($30 million) project that involved the implementation of SAP, which is a widely used enterprisewide computer system. The project took four years. Each year we started a new One-Page Project Manager. We changed the one-page project manager each year because the project took so long and was so complex that it changed or morphed significantly over its lifetime. It was impossible at the beginning of the project to know what the project—and therefore the one-page project manager—would look like years later. We just had to delve into the project, get on the mountain as it were, and react to the real world as it developed.

This variation on the one-page project manager is especially suited for information technology projects, including both hardware and software implementations. The owners have been divided into two groups: Business Leads (who are listed next to the Project list) and Technical Leads (in the right-hand side of the form). Business Leads are from the business side of the company (e.g., finance, production, and purchasing) and Technical Leads are the technical folks who implement the software and hardware.

In the matrices of other one-page project managers, there is a slice of the pie called Costs. Here, that slice is called Metrics because in an information technology project like this, some of what's being measured is in dollars, but there are other measurements, such as the percentage of orders filled on time, as well.

In the Finishing Cornerstone One-Page Project Manager, the color green explains that the part of the project in question is progressing on time and any current problems it has are manageable. Yellow says the project team is aggressively addressing difficult current problems, which are slowing progress. No additional help is needed to finish on time. Red says additional help is needed to attack extremely difficult problems, which are putting an on-time finish in jeopardy.

CARROTS CULTURE

This is the basic One-Page Project Manager format, adapted for a "carrots culture"—a corporate culture that uses employee recognition rewards strategically to strengthen the company. Employees become more engaged via the use of recognition awards, which are "carrots." The phrase *carrots culture* comes from a series of management/motivational books by Adrian Gostick and Chester Elton (who are both part of O.C. Tanner). Each book has the word "carrots" in its title: *The 24-Carrot Manager* (Layton, UT: Gibbs Smith, 2002) and *Managing with Carrots: Using Recognition to Attract and Retain the Best People* (Layton, UT: Gibbs Smith, 2001).

The object of a carrots culture—as in carrots versus sticks—is to attract, retain, and motivate employees. Human resources management focuses on three variables: compensation, benefits, and work experience. Managers generally have little leeway to tweak or adjust compensation and benefits. Therefore, managers can most influence the work experience, and this is where recognition awards play a vital role.

This One-Page Project Manager is a project tool to use over a two-year time horizon for companies looking to create a carrots culture in their organization to better engage their employees through a suite of valuable recognition tools.